LIVERPOOL

A Macabre Miscellany

Daniel K. Longman

AMBERLEY

With thanks to:

Owen Barton
Dorothy Bradwell
Matthew Dyer
HH Judge Clement Goldstone QC
Lyndsey-Jane Kevan
Robert T. H Owen JP DL

First published 2016

Amberley Publishing
The Hill, Stroud
Gloucestershire, GL5 4EP

www.amberley–books.com

Copyright © Daniel K. Longman, 2016

The right of Daniel K. Longman to be identified as the Author of this
work has been asserted in accordance with the
Copyrights, Designs and Patents Act 1988.

British Library Cataloguing in Publication Data.
A catalogue record for this book is available from the British Library.

ISBN 978 1 4456 4694 7 (print)
ISBN 978 1 4456 4695 4 (ebook)

Typesetting and Origination by Amberley Publishing.
Printed in Great Britain.

Contents

Foreword

As Honorary Recorder of Liverpool, I consider it a great honour to have been asked by Daniel Longman to pen a foreword to his book. The cases which he has carefully researched are classic examples of the many interesting, and sometimes confounding cases which have been tried in the Crown Court at Liverpool, and its predecessors, the Assize Court and Quarter Sessions. I am sure that the many distinguished Judges (among whom are included some of my illustrious predecessors) who presided over the cases which Daniel has selected for inclusion, would be impressed by, and approve of the way in which they have been skilfully recounted. I hope that those who read this book are able to obtain a sense of the atmosphere in which these cases were conducted; they amount to a significant contribution to the legal history of this great city.

HH Judge Clement Goldstone QC

Introduction

Liverpool's success has always attracted the great, the good, and indeed, the not so good.

We may be forgiven for thinking shocking headlines are a modern phenomenon, somehow alien to our ancestors who lived in for more innocuous times. This is a misconception. The media have always leapt at the chance to cover the outrageous and gruesome in their newsprints; bad news sells fast. In more recent years advances in technology has allowed all of us to become instant journalists, posting even the most mundane news to our social media accounts for all the world to see. We are able to tailor what we want to see and when we want to see it. The news is live and available at the touch of a button wherever it, and we, may be. Times have certainly changed from the era of newsrooms and reading libraries when updates could be sourced within the week. Those old reports frequently covered business and commercial matters, but they often included various tales of criminal misdemeanours and columns of miserable misfortune to rouse sensations of horror and delight. Many of those historic editions possessed detail to an unnecessary degree and by any standard were undoubtedly insensitive to the parties involved. Nevertheless, those long-gone journalists have allowed us to break through the limitations of time to discover the dark truth of the dreadfully tragic events of the past. Your imagination shall be needed to help embellish the scene, but judge for yourself the level of realism you wish to form in your mind's eye. The stories within are just a small selection of some of the more macabre and criminal events which took place within our city in times gone by. The people within have all passed on and until now memory of their existence had been lost with the demise of their generation. Good riddance to the miscreants and low-lives of those times, and may the law deal with the outright scum who persist in plaguing our society with their existence today. *Liverpool: A Macabre Miscellany* breathes life into the happenings of old, and reminds us of the hidden histories that once took place in the streets we call home. I hope you find the stories interesting, though perhaps not enjoyable, and that they provide an enlightening insight into events and goings on which may have otherwise been forgotten for the rest of time.

Daniel K. Longman JP

1. The Falling Barrel

On the Friday afternoon of 10 August 1832, Margaret Kearsley and her teenage daughter travelled to town from their house in Beau Street. Their day was spent happily enough until around three o'clock when the pair decided to make their way back home. Their route was nothing out of the ordinary but the events that were to take place were quite exceptional. The mother and daughter casually strolled down Dale Street and on arriving at the busy junction of Byrom Street they turned the corner and headed for home. In an instant their journey was cut short eternally, as an empty spirit cask plummeted from the sky flattening the females straight into the ground. It had fallen four storeys from Edward Rigmaiden's warehouse at the most inopportune moment. The barrel fell full force onto the head of the fifteen-year-old,

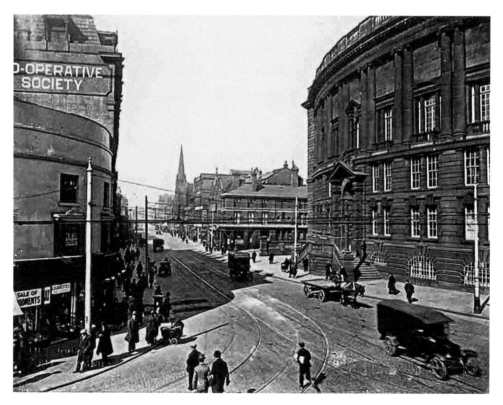

The junction of Bryom Street where the fatal incident occurred, seen *c.* 1910.

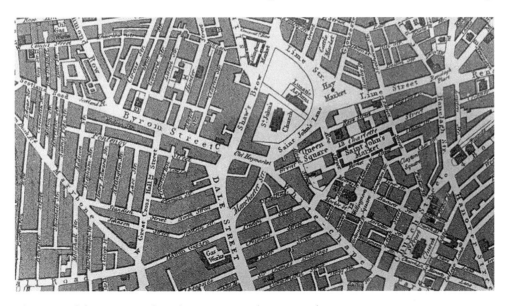

The scene of the tragic incident shown on an early nineteenth-century map.

cracking open her skull. Her mother fared no better as her scalp was sliced off during the affair, leaving her brain partially exposed. Neither had a chance to even cry out, but the younger Kearsley was seen to convulse silently as blood spewed from her eyes and mouth. Horrified city dwellers rushed to the rescue, but for the girl her short life was over. Her mother lingered for several minutes and was taken in her most ghastly state into a nearby druggist. The staff there were unable to treat such a grisly condition so she was carried straight to Mr Whitley's surgery back in Dale Street. Margaret was placed across two chairs and assisted by surgeon, Mr Black. Despite his efforts the forty-six-year-old died as a result of the terrible laceration evident upon her forehead. The distraught wine merchant Edward Rigmaiden was taken into custody on two charges of manslaughter and found guilty of the crimes at a sitting of the Lancaster Assizes. His testimony depicted a shocking tale of gross negligence and the jury heard how the fatal barrel had been secured only by a single rope and hoisted up in a somewhat improper manner. It was pure misfortune that the barrel struck the Kearsley family at that very moment and the case called into question the need for clear safety guidelines for warehousemen across the city. As for Edward's fate, he was strongly recommended to mercy and sentenced to only one month imprisonment at Lancaster Castle.

2. Hypnotic Neighbours

On Saturday 20 May 1899 the Liverpool authorities' attention was drawn to Kensington, in particular, a certain house in Adelaide Road. Their duty was to discover the cause of death of the local merchant Peter McArte, who was seventy-three years of age. Up until his passing the elderly gent had been living with his daughter Emily. She was thirty-eight years old and had been afflicted with a hostile form of mental illness for almost a decade. On the Tuesday of that week Miss McArte experienced a customary fit of violence and began aggressively throwing things into the backyard of her neighbour and smashed her front parlour windows. The occupier, Ann Roberts, was much aggrieved and called the police to prevent any more of this urban destruction. It was clear Miss McArte was a danger to others and quite possibly herself. Relieving Officer Mr Howard stated that in light of his child's latest bout of perilous behaviour Mr McArte had applied for her to be admitted to a lunatic asylum. The merchant presented a medical certificate as proof of her condition, but as a loving parent he struggled with the decision to commit her. Mr Howard told him that a place at the asylum would certainly be available to his daughter if he wished to proceed, and on the

No. 103 Adelaide Road, Kensington. Once the home of the McArtre family.

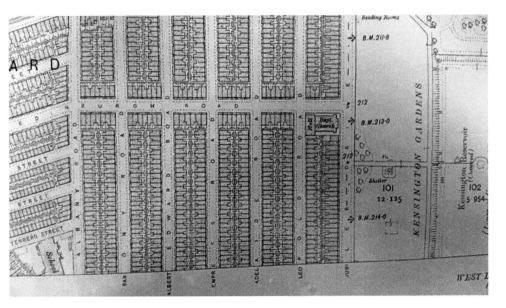

Adelaide Road as seen on a map form 1908.

facts of the medical evidence, strongly advised him to do so. Mr McArte mused about this prospect for some time but ultimately, he declined the offer. 'I will take her to the country for four or five weeks and see if it helps her,' he said. Mr McArte was warned that this was a particularly daring option, but nevertheless he politely sent Mr Howard on his way remarking that he would make his final decision in the morning. It was to be a morning that would never come.

Later that day police returned to the property, No. 103, and were shocked to discover the septuagenarian lying dead at the foot of the stairs in the lobby. His body was face down and bleeding from a wound to the forehead. When questioned, Ann told officers that the neighbours had hypnotised her father and taken away the power of his legs. She was promptly removed to the workhouse asylum. A subsequent post-mortem revealed that Peter had actually died from disease, but the mark on his forehead was caused at the time of death or immediately afterwards. It may have been caused by the fall or by a poker, but in the latter case it was surmised that blood would have been expected to be found on such an instrument. The inquest concluded that the death was due to natural causes. What happened to poor Ann McArte is unknown.

3. An Unbalanced Barman

A rather sensational affair took place at one Liverpool establishment back in the winter of 1892. It was around half-past ten at the Central Hotel, Ranelagh Street, when a young man of gentlemanly appearance entered the building through the main bar, passing into an adjoining room. Barmaid Amy Hughes followed with the intention of proposing some refreshment to the new guest, but she was horrified to discover that the man was brandishing a five-chambered revolver. He was in a most agitated state and with a trembling hand he raised the gun towards her. Amy shrieked and fled from the room to raise the alarm. Two loud shots rang out creating a public rush towards

Ranelagh Street as seen in the early twentieth century.

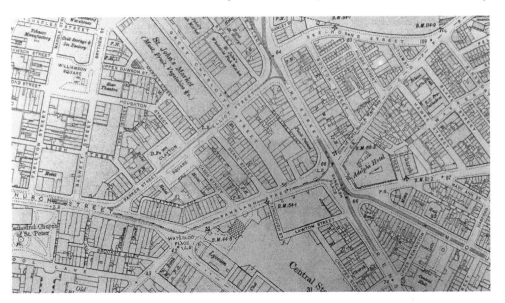

Ranelagh Street, the scene of the shooting on a map from the early twentieth century.

the source of the calamity. Drinkers Patrick Foley, William Walton, James McStemm and John McCabe dashed towards the deranged man but not before he had discharged the contents of the weapon into his own temple. He fell to the ground but the bullets did not achieve their fatal ambition – life was still quite evident. The Good Samaritan John McCabe had a lucky escape of his own: a stray bullet from the weapon passed by his chest by mere millimetres. The would-be fatality was carried out to the backyard of the hotel to await the help of the ambulance service who were racing to the scene. Subsequent investigations revealed that the attacker was Robert Golter, a barman residing on Wavertree's High Street. Dr Hare, who examined him at the hospital, found his wounds to be only superficial and it is presumed Robert made a full recovery. The reason for his bizarre and suicidal action was never disclosed.

4. A Despicable Delivery

On the evening of 15 February 1828 a young female traveller was on board the top deck of a carriage en route to Liverpool. She was labouring under the very advanced stages of pregnancy and with a baby due at any moment, she was keen to reach the city as fast as possible. The charging horses were heading for the Golden Lion Inn in Dale Street but on passing through Old Swan just a few miles from her destination, the woman felt immense pain and clutched her stomach in agony. The pain worsened still and it became clear this baby would wait for no one. Moments later the poor girl was forced to submit and give birth right there and then on top of the moving carriage. She screamed for the coachman to stop but he insensitively refused her cries for help. The heartless driver even declined to stop to allow the girl to climb into the inner carriage below, despite it being completely empty. As the horses galloped on through the night the struggling passenger was forced to endure the birth alone and pray to God for a safe delivery. On finally pulling into Dale Street later that night it was found that the girl had delivered a healthy male child whom she was embracing with great care. Both mother and child were helped to a friend's address in Johnson's Court, Edmund Street but not a hint of sympathy was expressed by the coachman. Had either of his passengers suffered fatal complications during his inhuman display of barbarity he would have no doubt have sworn innocence for his part in the woman's dreadfully traumatic journey.

By the time the woman reached Liverpool she had already given birth to a healthy baby boy.

The poor woman's terrible journey came to an end in Dale Street.

5. The Wicked Stepmother

Emma Welch had a truly awful life. As she stepped up into the dock Stipendiary Magistrate Mr Raffles braced himself to learn just how horrible her upbringing had been. The fourteen-year-old appeared very weak and undernourished for her age. She was the daughter of John, a compositor but she never knew her birth mother. Her stepmother however, also called Emma, had been in her life since her earliest memory. The girl stood to give evidence against her parents whom it was alleged mistreated her most cruelly for many years. She stated that at home she was never given regular meals and when she did get fed it was either dry bread and water or bread and butter. Emma said that she was never treated the same as her brothers and sisters. Frequently the child was made to sleep in the cellar, or sometimes on the stairs, and subjected to beatings. It was alleged that the stepmother often hit the girl with a cane and strap making her bleed. It was the usual punishment for when Emma was caught stealing food from shops in the neighbourhood, and who could blame her? When she tried to run away, the teen was made to wear boys' clothes in penance, and cold water thrown all over her. The court heard how Mr Welch also played a part in his daughter's nightmare, beating her with his strap and sometimes his boot. In regards to school, the child had been sent but was turned away for being what teachers described as incorrigible. 'They treated her like a wild beast and yet expected her to behave well,' remarked prosecutor Mr Marks. The witness added that her stepmother burnt her four times with a red-hot poker, and it was no accident. The poker was always made deliberately hot and applied once on her legs, another time on the hand, twice on her face near her eyes and another time she was burnt on the shoulders. To add to the malice, the stepmother would hit her wounds as they healed. On one occasion the girl was made to put her hands on top of the boiler while her guardian struck them with the blunt end of a chopper, breaking her knuckles. She was generally made to strip before the woman abused her. Emma held up her hands for all the court to see, the damage was evident. From February to April, the girl slept on the floor without any covering. Her recent salvation was only brought about when her father headed to bed drunk and was out like a light. As he slept, his sadistic wife bound the child's hands and feet together, then tied her to the bedpost to prevent any evening escape. As Mrs Welch slept soundly, Emma was able to bite through the rope that bound her and make a run for it.

Police took the girl to the Children's Shelter in Islington Square where she received a decent meal. The surroundings were familiar to Emma: she had been sent to the shelter two years earlier when her parents were cautioned as to their treatment of her.

Dr Evans, medical officer for the Liverpool Society for the Prevention of Cruelty to Children gave evidence of the absolute poverty Emma had suffered. He explained how a healthy girl of her age should weigh around 88 lbs, but when he admitted her she weighed only 48 lbs. He also observed multiple injuries, including broken fingers, old bruises and scars all over her body. He considered the child's general and mental health to have been permanently impaired by her experiences at the hands of her parents. During the trial Mr and Mrs Welch watched their daughter intently, sometimes audibly disputing the allegations against them. Both prisoners were committed to stand trial before Mr Justice Charles the following week, on 12 May 1888. During the early stages of the proceedings photographs of the victim were passed around the court. They showed the child in her most emaciated condition and with a sorrowfully gaunt expression that jurors were unlikely to forget. Ellen Divine's testimony revealed that she lived in Wellington Terrace, High Park Street where the accused had lived two years previously. She said that the girl was often kept in the cellar and was given food down there, but she was the only child to be put below ground. Mrs Divine said she had also seen Emma eating food in the parlour many times with her siblings and never saw her chastised any more than a normal mother would do.

Harry Ryder, aged eleven, said he lived at No. 12 Brighton Street. When the family lived in that street he used to play with their sons. It was three months before Harry realised there was a girl in the household. He had seen her eat bread and butter and the leftovers from the boys. The stepmother used to take them on a plate to the cellar and

Wellington Terrace, High Park Street, where the abused girl once lived.

The neighbourhood of High Park Street, where the Welch family resided.

shove them off a plate towards the girl. Whenever anyone went to the house Emma was rushed away to the cellar for shame.

Mary Billingsley, from No. 20 Brighton Street, said the prisoners lived next door to her for some time. The girl wore a pair of knickerbockers and a piece of rough wrapping. On one occasion Mary visited the property and saw the child crouching under a table, and she had a black eye. When Emma saw her come in, she hurried down into the cellar. The witness spoke of how she had often seen the other children of the family go to school in the mornings and they were all respectably dressed, but Emma was never among them. On other occasions Mary heard strange noises coming from the house as if someone was moaning on the stairs. She recalled experiencing this unusual noise for several days. One morning, after Mr and Mrs Welch had left the property, Mary went to investigate. She possessed a key for the purposes of letting and with a candle in hand made her way down to the cellar. She discovered that the shutters over the window had been nailed down tight, keeping the room in eternal darkness. Underneath the stairs there was a bed, emptied of stuffing with the outline of a child embossed into its form. She said that the cellar was in a filthy condition and in no way fit for human habitation.

Mrs Brough of Hawkstone Street told the court that in April the girl had come to her house and appeared much like she did in the photographs. She had visited several times over the past twelve months and always had black eyes and burns about her body. On one occasion Mrs Brough felt it necessary to keep the girl under her care for two weeks because she would not say where she lived. She was not well enough to go out and fainted every day. The kind neighbour took her to her friend Ann Wilson, who remarked that Emma was more like a monkey than a child.

Catherine Devine was next to assist the child and said that she had cooked Emma some steak and gave her tea but she fainted soon after eating, giving Catherine cause for concern. She contacted a doctor.

Dr Campbell told the court he was called to the house of Mrs Devine on 7 April to see a sickly girl. He found the patient to be suffering from stunted growth and an emaciated physical condition. The girl's clothing was in a dire state, fit only for the rubbish bin. The doctor also observed marks of violence, including a black eye, a sore over the left shoulder, the middle finger of the left hand swollen and stiff, and one of her fingers on the other hand was in a similar circumstance. Dr Campbell thought the child's intelligence to be lacking and she answered questions with great hesitation. In his opinion the girl was little more than skin and bone and very dirty.

Further evidence was provided by Dr Evans of the Society for the Prevention of Cruelty to Children, who in answer to the judge said that an injury he located, a bruise by the child's eye, must have been extremely violent and it was in a very dangerous region. A blow on the temple to a child of delicate health might even have caused death. The injuries were quite consistent with the account given by the girl.

Detective Richard Baxter gave evidence stating that he arrested the prisoners on 12 April and both protested their innocence. They had in fact come to the detective office to inquire about the health of their daughter, but he put the allegations to them and promptly put them away behind bars.

Mrs Welch told the jury she had cared for the girl since Emma was two years old and that she had always treated her as well as she treated the boys. She denied any of the events Emma had alleged, stating that if anything they had been too kind. Her husband said that all they had done was to be strict with the girl.

Judge Charles, in summing up to the jury, directed them only to discharge the accused couple if they believed that the evidence placed before them was a mass of trumped-up falsehood. Giving regard to the witness statements, the judge found it difficult to see how that conclusion could be reached.

The real and important question for the jury was on which two counts of the indictment should they be convicted: should they find the couple guilty of inflicting the injuries with intent to kill, or should they find them guilty of inflicting the injuries with intent to do grievous bodily harm? These were the only two alternatives on this occasion. However, the judge directed the jury that they should discriminate between the two prisoners. Both may have been guilty of inflicting the injuries upon the child with intent to kill, or only one may have wished to produce such a dark outcome. In other words, they may have been doing the same acts to the child, but yet, the intention to get rid of her might only have been in the mind of one. 'No amount of naughtiness on the part of the child could for a moment justify such horrible and inhuman acts. The jury must consider whether such acts if uninterrupted would likely lead to death,' said Judge Charles.

The jury considered their verdict and, in less than two minutes, found Mrs Welch guilty of doing grievous bodily harm with intent to murder and Mr Welch of grievous bodily harm with intent.

> Sarah Ruth Welch, the jury have convicted you, and in my opinion, most properly convicted you, of causing grievous bodily harm to this unfortunate child with intent to kill her. This girl may have been a naughty girl, she may have been a wicked girl, or she may have been a dishonest girl, but no one of these faults could for a moment justify the horrible and inhumane brutality with which you have treated her. I must inflict upon you the maximum sentence which the law allows. I order you to be kept in penal servitude for life.

The woman seemed somewhat staggered as she was led away by two warders below. The judge next addressed the second prisoner:

> John Welch, the jury have taken a more merciful view of your case but you are indeed deeply guilty. You are the father of this unfortunate little creature, and you saw her being, I had almost said, done to death before your eyes without interfering, but the jury, and rightly so I may say again, have taken a merciful view of your conduct and have come to the conclusion that although you concurred in some of these brutal acts done, you did not concur fully in them; therefore they have found you guilty of grievous bodily harm to this unfortunate child, your own girl, not with the intent to kill but to do grievous bodily harm. I sentence you to be kept in penal servitude for seven years.

'Perhaps the witnesses are now satisfied!' growled the prisoner as he too descended to the cells.

6. A Discovery at the Docks

A rather distressing discovery was reported in the summer of 1866 when the remains of a missing youngster were sorrowfully located. On the Thursday afternoon of 12 July, seaman John Coy was working aboard the steamboat *Lioness* when something extraordinary caught his gaze. Looking out from the vessel down into the waves he spotted an unusual object floating in the choppy waters. It washed limply against the wall of the Albert Dock and appeared to be quite lifeless. Closer scrutiny by all those on board brought about the sad revelation that it was the body of a young boy. The crew of the *Lioness* towed the saturated corpse across the river and landed it at the Seacombe slip where officials were notified. The body was soon taken to the Princes Dock dead house where it was found to be the remains of the missing Gilbert Angers. The nine-year-old had vanished from his home in Frank Street, Toxteth Park the previous week much to the anguish of his father Peter Angers, a sailor, and the rest of his inconsolable family. An inquest was held by Deputy Coroner Devey but no evidence could be ascertained as to how poor Gilbert found himself in the heartless waters of the Mersey. A verdict of 'Found Drowned' was returned.

The child's saturated body was found in waters close to the Albert Dock.

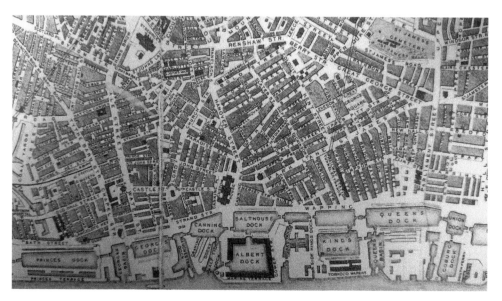

Liverpool's docks seen here on a contemporary map.

7. The Priest of Princes Park

On Thursday 20 July 1882, little Charlotte Henderson returned to her home at No. 40 Greta Street and cried for her father. She had been playing in nearby Princes Park with friends when something awful had happened. Charlotte's skirt dripped with blood and the five-year-old complained of pain. Mr Henderson ordered his wife to take Charlotte to a doctor immediately.

It transpired that earlier that afternoon Charlotte, her elder brother Alex and some friends had been playing on the grass when a man had approached the group and sat down beside them. He held a large umbrella which he duly opened, then said 'Won't some of you little girls come and sit under my umbrella, and we will have a little summer house.' Anne Sims, one of the more mature youngsters replied politely that they would not and quickly left the group to go find a policeman.

In her absence the peculiar playmate took hold of little Charlotte and placed her down firmly next to him. He then asked Alex to go off and fetch some matches for him. On being handed the money the young lad naively went off to the nearest shop, leaving the strange man alone with the girls.

During the moments that followed a most disgusting assault took place beneath the clandestine cover of the umbrella, something that would surely scar the innocent child forever.

A short while later Anne returned having been unable to find a policeman. The deviant reached into his pocket and offered her £2 if she would now sit beside him. Her answer was a resounding no. Alex also returned to the park and handed over the box of matches as requested.

The man took the box, stood up from the grass and swiftly headed out of the park. It was then that Anne saw a policeman walking by and alerted him to the strange character and obvious distress he had caused to little Charlotte. The officer scoured the area but could find no sign of the sinister attacker.

The following afternoon the same officer was back on his beat and spotted a curious individual matching the description of the assailant given to him by the other children. He also remembered seeing the man in the vicinity before the incident so was virtually certain he had the right man. Once again he was behaving in a suspicious manner.

'You have not the same trousers upon you as you had yesterday?' remarked the officer, as he questioned the man. 'No. My grey trousers are in my valise at the North Western Hotel.' The officer explained that he was searching for a man matching his description and the allegation was put to him. He gave his name as forty-year-old Patrick Pacificus Wade, a Roman Catholic priest stationed in Darlington. 'Don't detain me; I am on my

Princes Park was the scene of Father Wade's disgraceful actions.

holidays and have to officiate on Sunday. I have been drinking and do not remember what passed. If I did so it is against what I have been teaching and against my principles.'

The constable was satisfied that he had apprehended the correct suspect and during a search a box of matches was found, identical to the description given by Alex Henderson. The constable escorted the prisoner to the station.

Due to the very serious nature of this matter magistrates committed the case to Crown Court where on 4 August Father Patrick stood trial for the rape of five-year-old Charlotte Henderson. It was revealed that on the evening of the alleged offence he had stayed the night at the property of a disreputable woman, who believed him to be a married bank manager from Newcastle away on business. The case against Father Patrick's dubious character was mounting.

On hearing the precise but terrible details of the incident, it was agreed that the offence alleged was incorrect and an alternative charge of indecent assault would be more appropriate. To this, the defendant pleaded guilty. 'On the evidence I cannot say anything else but that I am guilty. But I must say that I have no knowledge of what I did.'

In his defence Mr Potter QC stated that his client had been for some years in California and had come back invalided. Since that time he had been at home and had been in his present condition for four years. During that period he had conducted himself well, but owing to the effect of the climate in which he had resided, the taking of even a moderate amount of drink affected him in a very serious manner and he was not fully conscious of what he was doing on the day in question.

Judge North declared that the prisoner had pled guilty to an offence shocking to any man, but worse when committed by a minister of religion. Father Patrick was sentenced to two years' imprisonment with hard labour.

The setting for depravity – Princes Park, as shown on a map dating from 1891.

8. The Lime Street Fireworks

On 27 October 1868, firefighters rushed to the scene of No. 48 Lime Street after receiving reports of a building ablaze. The property alight was particularly flammable: one half was set up for the sale of fireworks, the other for cigars and tobacco. By some awful calamity the contents of the shop caught alight and so began a series of explosive indoor detonations. An unwelcome display of noise, colour and light was forced into action as one by one, fireworks burst menacingly into life. The ensuing inferno was quite a sight to roadside onlookers but its tangible effects were far from amusing.

Witnesses were astounded to see the owner, Mr Bradbury, rush out of the shop with a lit firework still in his grasp. This singular action would make no difference now. Firemen and salvage officers fought in earnest to supress the rainbow blaze in an effort to save the building from complete and utter ruin. With their hoses hooked to the hydrants water gushed forth into the burning shop, but it was still unclear whether anyone was still trapped inside. The volatile stock gave the fire a considerably ferocious spirit and it quickly became obvious that the brigade was fighting a losing battle. So violent was the disaster the window of an adjoining shop was completely blown out and its own stores damaged by water.

When the flames were eventually supressed, salvage officers hurried into the building and made the discovery the team was dreading. In the rear hallway they found the body of a boy. This was Christopher Kelly, a youthful customer who had the misfortune to be in the wrong place at the wrong time. He was discovered facedown with his head against a door leading to an exit. Every piece of clothing, but for his boots, had been burnt from his body. His face, head, arms, legs and torso were completely calcined from the intense heat, making any of his human features nearly impossible to distinguish. The remains were carefully wrapped in a rug and placed in a room at the back of the shop. A subsequent inquest failed to determine the cause of the occurrence but recommended that firework sellers should in future operate under the strict supervision of the authorities.

The old properties of Lime Street have since been replaced.

Lime Street depicted on a mid-nineteenth-century map.

9. Pushed to the Edge

Forty-four-year-old pavier John Hitchmough lodged at No. 7 Reservoir Street with his wife Ellen. He enjoyed a drop to drink but by the November of 1867 he had given up alcohol completely. His health however was extremely poor and on the Sunday of the 24th the poor man suffered no less than sixteen epileptic fits. On the Monday he remained in bed all day feeling ill and exhausted. On the Tuesday he arose and came downstairs for breakfast. 'Don't be afraid wench, I shall be all right after that sickness,' he muttered, as he paced about the living room.

Later that day John put on his coat and hat and asked his wife to go for a walk with him. She declined saying that it was too cold to go outside, especially as he had not been well the past two days. Instead, Mrs Hitchmough read some religious tracts for him

John and Ellen Hitchmough's former residence of Reservoir Street.

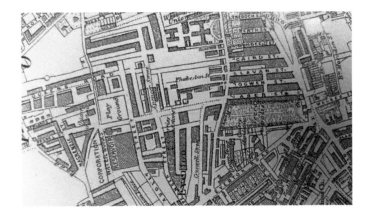

The locality seen on a contemporary nineteenth-century map.

to try and settle his nerves. Mr Hitchmough was acting highly unusual but he assured her repeatedly not to be afraid. He continued to sit in an upstairs room in his coat and hat refusing to take them off, despite his wife's best efforts. Ellen went out to fetch a neighbour who might be able to persuade her husband to get back in bed and wait for his illness to pass; he was certainly not acting like his usual self. While downstairs, Ellen heard the sound of a window opening, so quickly ran back to see if her husband was alright. On reaching the room she found John had fastened the door shut from the inside. With all her might, Mrs Hitchmough managed to force her way into the room and to her dismay found the floor covered in blood. She saw John sitting on the window ledge looking down into the street. The tendons of his neck were partially exposed from a self-inflicted wound with a razor blade. Ellen ran to the window and attempted to drag her husband back into the room, but he broke free of her grip and fell 13 feet to the pavement. A crowd of neighbours who had heard the commotion gathered around the property and several helped carry Mr Hitchmough back into the house to await medical help. Sadly the man died before doctors could reach him and at a subsequent inquest, a verdict of suicide while in a state of temporary insanity was returned.

10. Rajah the Elephant

Liverpool's own zoological gardens, built on a huge plot of land just off West Derby Road, opened its doors for the first time in 1833. It featured a variety of exotic creatures including lions, llamas and zebras never before seen by captivated crowds. Over a decade later on the morning of 17 June 1848 the great Rajah, a thirty-five-year-old elephant caused a sensation by crushing his keeper to death. It was then that zoo attendant, Richard Howard, had been brushing out the animal's den and had ordered Rajah to move aside. This, the animal failed to do, so Mr Howard issued further encouragement with a sharp tap with his broom. An angry growl filled the enclosure as Rajah became infuriated, forcing his keeper up against the iron bars of the pen. The immense weight of the creature left little hope of survival and upon Rajah retreating Mr Howard slumped to the ground, his body crushed appallingly with an array of compound fractures. Certain death drew near as the ponderous power of the elephant's foot came down carelessly upon the poor man's already inert body. It was an unquestionable end. The alarm was raised and it was agreed to bring the animal down by poisoning. A concoction of prussic acid, aconite and treacle failed to have the desired effect so the order for two dozen rifle men to enter the den was given. They discharged their bullets into the elephant which slumped to the ground within moments. Its carcass was left out for public display before dissection, while the body of Mr Howard was taken away to await a formal inquest. He left behind a wife and two children.

The destruction of Rajah the elephant was captured in the *Illustrated London News*, 1845.

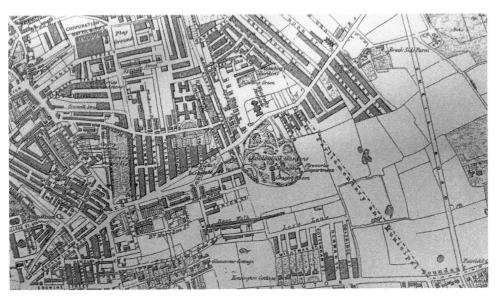

The site of the Zoological Gardens as shown on a map dating from 1863.

11. Buried Alive

On the warm Tuesday evening of 12 June 1860, gardener Thomas Harris began his usual walk home from a day's hard work. His attention was caught by juvenile cries coming from a small shrubbery bush in Anfield Road, cries that his conscience begged him to investigate. When Thomas knelt down beside the bush he noticed a small area of soil had been disturbed and appeared to be somewhat raised and uneven. He brushed away the sods and buried beneath he found a baby girl, alive but extremely exhausted. Her mouth was filled with soil and dirt and the girl was struggling to breath. The gardener carefully removed the filth from the baby's mouth

Anfield Road seen in modern times.

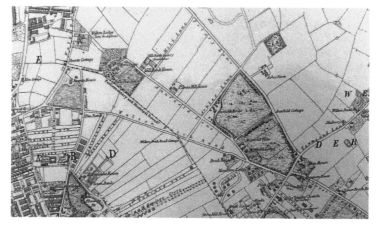

The vicinity of Anfield Road where the baby was buried, shown on a historical map.

before carrying the pitiful infant to the nearest police station. From there it was taken into the care of the midwife at the West Derby Workhouse, who due to some unusual marks recognised the child to be the daughter of Ann Murphy. The twenty-seven-year-old had only recently been an inmate at the institution and had given birth to a baby girl during her time there. An urgent search for Ann's whereabouts commenced.

Later that night at a lodging house in Beau Street the woman was found and sternly questioned as to the location of her newborn. Ann denied any wrongdoing, stating that the baby was now safely on its way to live with relatives in Glasgow. Her dubious answers stank of suspicion and she was charged with the attempted murder of her own daughter. On the way to Old Swan Police Station Ann finally confessed: 'I am sorry that I have done it. I have murdered the child.' Little did she know the baby was still alive and fighting for its life. It became apparent that on the Monday morning Ann had been supplied with clothes for the child and allowed to leave the workhouse. A portion of these clothes were later found to have been pledged and the child dressed meagrely in a handful of old rags. It was these in which the baby was found when Thomas Harris discovered her buried alive. By that point the infant had lain there for approximately three hours. At a Crown Court sitting on 14 August Miss Murphy awaited sentencing. In her defence Ann pleaded that she had no means of supporting her child and did not know what she was doing at the time of the interment. Fortunately for her, the child had survived and Ann was found guilty of the lesser charge of common assault. For this she was given four months imprisonment with hard labour.

12. Under the Bridge

An inquest into the death of Thomas Ball was held at the Willowbank Hotel, Smithdown Road, in the spring of 1893. Enquiries into the passing revealed that the deceased was fifty years of age, a boilermaker and up to his demise had resided at Upper Essex Street in Toxteth. Thomas had been reported as missing by his family a whole week before his body was discovered hanging lifelessly from a bridge in the luscious greenery of Sefton Park. A young lady out walking had the misfortune to make the awful discovery after noticing a lone coat resting suspiciously under the bridge. Upon gazing upward she screamed as the pale cadaver that was Thomas Ball dangled hauntingly above her. Mr Bevan, a park keeper, cut down the body and Police Constables Blackburn and Young transferred it to Fever Hospital Mortuary. It was revealed that the man had been suffering from depressed spirits of late and had previously been an inmate of the Rainhill Asylum. On 4 April Coroner Brighouse returned a verdict of suicide while temporarily insane.

The bridge of Sefton Park, where a young lady discovered the body.

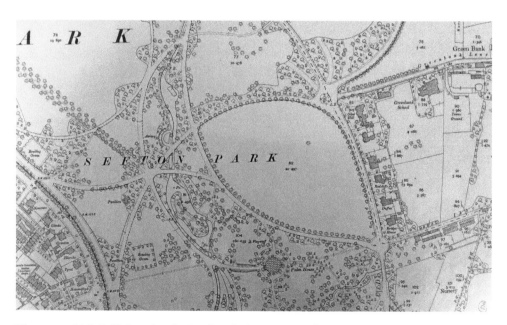

The scene of Mr Ball's hanging depicted in the late nineteenth century.

13. The Constable Killer

On the night of 15 April, a little before 10.00 p.m., Police Constable David Bailey, No. 388 was on patrol of Section Two and had the thirteenth beat. Section Two comprised of the Hanover Street district including College Lane, the side street in which Constable Bailey found himself patrolling that fateful night. Robert Rigg was a master mariner and in his maritime garb he made a common sight as he too walked along College Lane.

'Lovely night' remarked Mr Rigg cheerfully as he passed Officer Bailey on the sidewalk. The two men chatted over the unusually tranquil weather as they walked leisurely together towards Peter Lane.

Meanwhile, over in Green's Court, the scene was distinctly less serene. It was there that thirty-year-old Daniel Cole was returning home to his lodgings. He was heavy set and a powerful-looking man, standing at around five feet ten with thick broad shoulders and a deep black moustache. He gave off an impression of a somewhat fearsome temperament to all who laid their eyes upon him. Despite his thuggish appearance Daniel was usually a quiet individual, hardworking and

A depiction of Hanover Street by the Victorian artist W. G. Herdman.

industrious. The house in which he lodged was owned by Mrs Mary Moran, a widow who lived with her daughter Frances and several other lodgers, including Daniel's troublesome and trying wife. Mrs Cole was known to the police as an occasional street walker and a woman to be of decidedly drunken habits, but Daniel was no angel: he had previously been known to the courts on account of a previous stabbing incident.

That evening saw Mrs Cole indulge in more than enough to drink and her condition became one of utter intoxication. In the room was Mrs Moran and Alice Murphy, a fellow lodger who was on good terms with the Cole couple and Mrs Moran. 'You had better go to bed my good woman, for if your husband comes in I am afraid you will catch it,' said Mary, as she made up a bed by the fireplace. She had her back to the door laying down sheets on a mattress when Daniel entered the room. He observed Mrs Murphy kneeling at the fireplace. It had become quite dark in the small living quarters so Alice knelt down and lighted a candle at the fire. The distinctive smell of smoke wafted about the small living room as the drunken Mrs Cole extinguished the flame with her forefinger and thumb, and giggled. Mrs Murphy relit the wax column but the drunken woman persisted in her wit and jokingly put it out again. Daniel became furious. On several occasions he had returned from work to such alcoholic scenarios and he was sick of it. 'What's your humour for quenching the candle?' He realised that she had once again been drinking. 'Is that the way again lassie?' Daniel despaired. 'Dan, I'm not drunk; I'm not drunk!' she argued drunkenly. 'Stand up then, directly.' With all the grace of a newly-born giraffe, Mrs Cole carefully prepared to stand aloft from her seat, but all of a sudden her balance was lost and she tumbled backwards into the corner of the room looking very dishevelled and her eyes all ablur. Mrs Murphy helped the tenant

The shabby court dwelling of the Coles no longer exists.

to her feet and moved some of the now upturned chairs out of the way. Mrs Cole staggered to the kitchen where her husband was now standing in a growing state of intolerance. As an inner red mist clouded his eyes he made an impatient strike at his wife in the neck, stepping back a few paces soon afterwards. Mrs Cole at once realised that she had been stabbed and blood trickled steadily down her throat. This sobering act sent Mrs Cole out of the room running and down the court with her apron pressed against her neck.

'You villain! You have cut her neck!' seethed Mrs Moran. She had only known the Coles for three weeks and was shocked at the nature of Daniel's unexpected burst of untameable aggression. 'Murder! Police! A man has cut his wife's throat!' It was these terrifying words that reached the ears of Constable Bailey and Robert Rigg as they neared the corner of Peter Lane. Adrenaline began to pump. PC Bailey wasted no time. He requested assistance from mariner Rigg who, with subtle bravado, was happy to oblige and the pair ran off to the source of the cries.

Local shoemaker Manlove Moulson had been at his home at the bottom of the court when a lodger from Mrs Moran's came knocking urgently for help. Mr Moulson answered and on hearing news of the incident Moulson, his daughter Ann, and her friend Frances Moran ran out the back door and out onto Green's Court. It was there that Mrs Cole walked unsteadily along the street calling for a doctor as she clasped a red, dripping hand tightly around her throat.

Ann and Frances went up to the door of the Moran residence and could see that Daniel Cole was still in the house. Mrs Moran was in no uncertain terms admonishing him as a murderous villain and scoundrel. A quantity of Mrs Cole's blood lay in a glutinous puddle at their feet.

The scene of Constable Bailey's killing in Hanover Street.

The cobbles of College Lane were soon pounded by the boots of Officer Bailey, mariner Rigg and Mr Moulson as they entered the squalor of the urban court. At once Constable Bailey looked through the door. Daniel Cole was within, but he was a huge man; certainly no match for a single officer. The three entered the backyard of the property where Bailey charged his two amateur assistants with keeping Mr Cole in the house while he raced off to find some fellow officers for help in the arrest. It was now up to Rigg and Moulson to stand at the door to prevent the malevolent man's escape. Almost immediately Robert scolded the rogue for his recent actions, a remark that caused Daniel to come out into the yard and try to take flight. The mariner shoved him back with a hard push to the chest before rapidly closing the door in his face. He and Moulson fought hard to keep the door shut but Mr Cole was proving too powerful. The two men valiantly held the fort but in the end their foe proved too strong. Mr Moulson ran off to find the constable before it was too late. There was no way they would be able to restrain their prisoner if he escaped, and he was soon proved right. The door gave way and before he knew it the lone seaman was on the ground nursing a blow to the right cheek. Soon enough he was down again with a second as Daniel Cole ran off out of the court to make his escape. Sporting a reddening and bloody bruise across the face Rigg dusted himself off and gave chase.

Several members of the public shouted over to the pursuer and informed in of the direction his assailant had ran. Others called out to PC Bailey who was now in Hanover Street. 'Policeman, this is the way he has gone!' By the time Robert had got to the corner of College Lane Daniel had reached the opposite side of Hanover Street near to the Excise Office. PC Bailey was following close behind with his trusty nightstick in hand. He was halfway across Hanover Street with his left hand up at shoulder height, about to make a grab at Cole, when Ann Moulson let out a gut-wrenching warning, 'Oh dear, he's got a knife! Mind him, take care, he'll kill someone!' PC Bailey misjudged his distance and sped several paces ahead of his target. He turned and attempted to take a hold, but Cole was quick to strike with truly tragic consequences. Constable Bailey raised his truncheon but he soon felt the ice cold metal of a knife pressed into his neck. As the wound seeped its crimson content he put a trembling hand up to his left side in horror and began to stagger backwards. The crazed offender raised his weapon a second time to hit the officer again. He was only prevented by Robert Rigg, who wrestled the reprobate to the ground seemingly with no fear for his own safety. The desperate scuffle that commenced sent both men to the cobbles with David Bailey all the while staggering backwards into the road. He was striking his staff hard against the increasingly bloodstained flagstones in panic. His loud repetitive thud for help echoed through the night as the left side of the constable's neck was bleeding like a waterfall. Witnesses would later state that they could actually hear the patter of the blood as it hit the pavement.

Ann Moulson with the help of Seel Street resident Jane Greason and local man Charles Dogherty, ran across the street to give the constable some much needed support. He was able to walk for approximately 4 or 5 yards before his legs gave way and collapsed beneath him. With great haste they carried the officer to Jason Atherton's public house over in the now notorious College Lane and called for the vital medical expertise of a doctor. The victim's attacker Daniel Cole was arrested by several police officers who had eventually reached the hectic scene of the crime. They found him pinned to the ground by a number of people, one being Thomas Fletcher, a watchmaker from Richmond Row who had been in the vicinity when the commotion broke out. He had successfully secured Cole's legs with the help of passer-by James McCluskie, while Mr William Selsby removed the tarnished weapon from their thrashing prisoner's right hand.

Three constables, Gregory, Jones and Ferguson took hold of the attacker and walked him up to the Hotham Street Bridewell. They were assisted by Hugh McCree who noticed that Daniel was very calm on the journey, and even said that if the men would take him honourably he would stay quiet. 'Yes, you deserve to be treated honourably after sticking a knife to a man!' retorted Hugh sarcastically. 'Yes and I'd do the same to you' Cole answered, and his behaviour became so rebellious and coarse that the officers were forced to offer him several smacks with their batons to shut him up. At the bridewell a now silent Cole was handed over into the custody of keeper John Thursby along with a number of pieces of evidence, including a muddy and bloodstained clasp knife and Constable Bailey's helmet. Daniel would now have to await his destiny behind the bars of the Hotham Street lock-up before his trial.

Over in College Lane Constable Bailey was dead. He left a wife and two children. Dr John Callan, a Duke Street surgeon and his assistant Dr Peter McIntyre had arrived at Jason Atherton's pub a little after 10.00 p.m. and found to their dismay that David Bailey had already perished. It was their estimation that death would have occurred within five minutes of the stab wound being inflicted. Two days later the pair and their colleague Dr Cooper examined the wound in greater detail and found that the knife had penetrated the skin under the left ear, dividing all the main arteries and even the jugular vein. So severe had been the force of the assault the blade had actually pierced through the tongue and struck against the officer's inner right jawbone. The experts agreed that this wound was quite sufficient to cause the fatality of which PC Bailey had suffered. This now appeared to be a case of murder.

On the morning of Tuesday 20 August, Daniel Cole's crime finally came under the scrutiny of the Crown Court. His judge was to be Justice Coltman who arrived at 9.00 a.m. to a greatly crowded courtroom. In a white moleskin suit Mr Cole was called to stand and give his plea. In a firm voice he answered, 'Not guilty'. The details of the murderous matter were dissected before the twelve admirable gentlemen of the jury with evidence heard from members of the Moran household, their neighbours, the deceased's fellow officers, and those who were unlucky enough to be walking in the Hanover Street area that atrocious April evening.

Also to give evidence was Michael Cole, the prisoner's brother. He attested to the facts that Daniel had lived in Liverpool for about twelve years and before that he had lived in Ireland. It was one detail in particular though that members of the court played close attention to. Michael said:

> Sometime previous to coming to Liverpool … he worked with me at a quarry. He was in the habit of blasting coals. I recollect, upon one occasion, when he was blasting being wounded on the head and was confined for several weeks. After this he got injured again on his head while blasting; one of his eyes was damaged and he has nearly lost the sight of it. He was confined to the infirmary for a great number of weeks. He always wore tight bandages around his head and from that time I have never considered him in the right mind.

If the prisoner was indeed suffering from a mental illness then there may have been just cause for the charge of murder to be reduced. Of Mrs Cole, who had since recovered from her wound after stumbling into Mr Taylor's surgery in Cleveland Square that night, Michel Cole held a very dim view. He described her as a very drunken woman who frequently went off on three or four day benders spending Daniel's hard-earned wages. 'I have known her to sell the provisions out of the house for the purpose of procuring liquor. I have even known her when he has been in my house to throw stones through the window' said the second Mr Cole. When Mrs Cole behaved in this manner Michel said that his brother would become deranged and be obliged to have his head bound tight in bandages. He would take a fit and struggle so much that it required two or three men to hold him still.

> After the fits are over he cannot recollect anything which he has done under the influence. I had frequently told him of things he had done and he would not believe me. When he has been so excited he has frequently assaulted me and I have seen him break all the furniture in the house with an axe. He made a kick at me and struck his wife … and I wish he had killed her that day.

That was the end of Michel Cole's disposition. Mr Armstrong, prosecuting, took his chance to question the witness and asked the Irishman to further explain the violent fits that his brother seemed to suffer from. Michael admitted that on the occasions he had just mentioned Daniel was so excited he had taken to drink, but even when his wife was sober and he was drunk, Daniel would always behave peacefully. If he saw his wife drunk however then he would break into a rage. 'He has asked me when sober, on being told of his violence why I did not tie his head tight. This always had the tendency of quietening him. When his head was not tied he remained violent as long as any person crossed him.'

Jeremiah Levi gave a character reference of Daniel Cole and stated that he had worked with him for around eight years at a warehouse in which the men were employed as porters. Mr Levi had always considered Daniel to be a steady, sober man, and a faithful servant to his employer. Differing testimony came from James McDonald with whom the accused had worked occasionally for around five years. He believed Daniel to be a decent and trustworthy man but noticed that when he took to drink it deranged him. 'From his conduct after taking liquor I always considered him out of his mind' said James.

There appeared to be no doubt in Judge Coltman's mind that the deceased had died as a result of the consequences of the stabbing. Considering all the evidence that had been put before them, the jury had to decide as to the exact nature of the offence that had been committed. The judge was keen to remind them that it might have been possible for the accused to have been in a deranged state of mind at the time of the killing and therefore not accountable for the act. Conversely, if they believed Mr Cole was in control of his brutal actions, then was his crime one of murder or merely manslaughter? Did the prisoner intend to kill Officer Bailey? After some further thoughtful remarks by his Lordship into the nature of the law, the gentlemen of the jury retired to deliberate a verdict. They remained away from court for forty-five minutes and upon returning to their seats the foreman was addressed by Judge Coltman:

'How do you find the prisoner?'

'We find the prisoner guilty of a very aggravated case of manslaughter, my Lord.'

'Prisoner at the bar, you have been found guilty of a most aggravated manslaughter; one so nearly allied to murder, that it is only in the slightest degree distinguishable. Fortunately for you that slight distinction has been drawn. If the jury had been of the opinion that capital charge had been established it would have been my painful duty to have left you for execution.'

Daniel Cole breathed a huge sigh of relief. His life would be spared.

'It is a case in which the life of one of the police offices of the town has been sacrificed by that most base mode of death, stabbing, which I am sorry to find, is of late much on the increase.'

Daniel's heart was still pounding and he knew that he would still face a strict punishment for his actions.

'The penalty to which you are liable,' announced Judge Coltman 'and which it is my duty to pronounce upon you is that you be transported beyond the seas to such a place as her Majesty, by the advice of her Privy Council, may determine, for the term of your natural life.'

Daniel Cole was then led away.

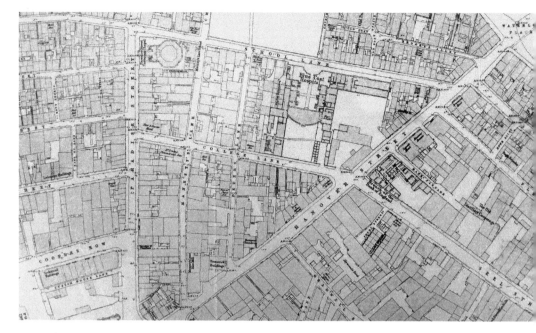

The neighbourhood of Hanover Street where Constable Bailey met his end.

14. The Fate of Benjamin Capon

An inquest held at the Stanley Arms in Roby examined the death of seventy-three-year-old Benjamin Capon. It was said how on 6 October 6 1899 the deceased left his home at No. 104 Vine Street, appearing to be in his typical state of health. He lived with his daughter and on that afternoon bid her goodbye before embarking on his usual walk. As can be expected for a man of his age, Mr Capon was not as sprightly as he once was. He had retired from his job as a merchant manager three years previously owing to ill-health and lately Mr Capon had seemed a little more forgetful. Nevertheless there seemed no real cause for concern. As the hours passed on and still no sign of the elderly man's return his family began to fear the worse. Testimony was heard from Arthur Crawford, a teamsman for Farmer Burton of Pilch Lane. He said that on returning home with his wife that night he had seen Mr Capon standing by a gate at around midnight. 'I spoke to the man several times but he made no answer' said Arthur. The next day the body of Benjamin was found floating in a pond on Page Moss Farm. There was no evidence to suggest how or why Mr Capon was in Roby that day as his only link to the area was his former employer. After a short deliberation the jury returned an unenlightening verdict of 'Found Drowned'.

The site of the Page Moss Farm pond is now occupied by twentieth-century houses.

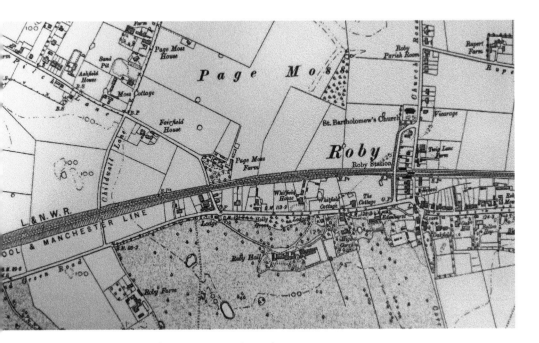

Page Moss Farm in Roby as shown on a map from the 1890s.

15. A Skeletal Sight

Rumours of a despicable murder spread like wildfire in the September of 1846 after a gang of inquisitive boys playing in a disused quarry made an a deathly discovery. It was their macabre misfortune to notice certain skeletal body parts within the old Prescot Street pit, including thigh bones, a spine, shoulder blades, and a skull. All of these appeared relatively free from damage except the cranium which exhibited several fractures. Worried residents in the area soon began to fear a criminal cover-up to have taken place, but on further examination by officials it was found that a number of the bones were connected by internal wires. This strongly hinted that the fleshless corpse was once the fitting property of some student of anatomy and the hunt for a killer was averted. It was said that several years before, a local surgeon who had worked up a huge debt to his landlord and other creditors found himself unable to pay the bills. In haste the medical man had gathered up his belongings and ran from the city in the dead of night. It is supposed his skeletal companion was too cumbersome to join him for the escape and was reluctantly thrown into the quarry below.

Prescot Street as seen in more recent times.

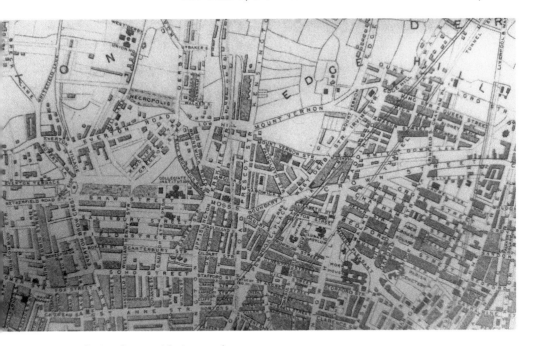

Prescot Street depicted on a mid-nineteenth-century map.

16. Wide of the Wicket

Twenty-two-year-old John Viccars was a keen sportsman and on Saturday 12 August 1871 he was asked to compete in a game of early evening cricket. Along with his teammates of the Arckles Cricket Club the young men met up in Stanley Park and were all eager to begin play and thrash the visiting rivals. John was up for batting and he prepared to strike. With his body posed to smash the ball off into the horizon he waited for the pitch. This came from Joseph Gregory who confidently launched the ball onto its speeding trajectory. However, it bounced off the grass and flew up at John's head, striking him hard on the right temple. Grimacing in pain the young architect seemed rather stunned by the blow and took several minutes to regain his composure. After a short break John was able to play on for a further forty-five minutes until a sudden splitting headache rendered the game over. He was taken back home to No. 15 Northumberland Terrace in Everton where John made light of the incident to his concerned parents. 'I'll be fine' John said, and he retired to bed at his usual time at around 9.00 p.m. The next morning his absence from breakfast was an immediate worry. He was found in bed unconscious. Doctor Burrows was called in and he applied a multitude of remedies, but in the end he had no choice but to declare the patient dead shortly after noon that day. The fatality was later recorded as accidental death.

Stanely Park was the scene of the ill-fated cricket match.

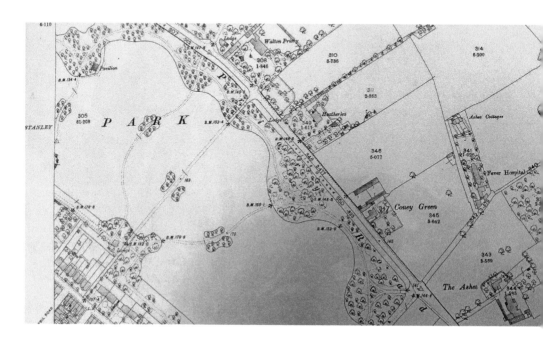

A map of Stanley Park, where John Viccars played his final game.

17. The Final Curtain

The Thursday afternoon of 12 January 1905 witnessed the inquest of theatre-goer Alfred Williams, who perished during a festive performance at the Rotunda Theatre. The previous week Mr Williams had gone along to the Rotunda, situated at the junction of Scotland Road and Stanley Road, with his children and mother-in-law. The pantomime season was drawing to a close but a production of *Aladdin* was still tempting in the crowds. During the performance Alfred suddenly leaned forward and pointed, exclaiming 'That is my wife!' and upon uttering the final syllable he fell to the floor in a state of inertia. Theatre attendants raised the lights and the man was carried out for

The Rotunda Theatre, the scene of Mr Williams' fatality.

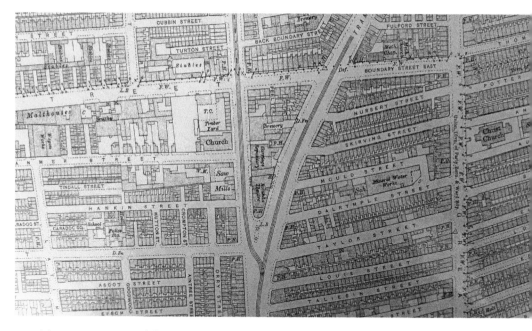

The prominent site of the Rotunda Theatre seen on a map from early 1900s.

urgent medical checks. He was however, already dead. Discussions at the inquest revealed how thirty-three-year-old Williams had lived apart from his wife for some time, and upon seeing who he thought to be his spouse on stage he became wildly animated. It was agreed that Williams' death was due to syncope, brought about by excitement. Mrs Williams, the deceased's widow was also in attendance for the proceedings. She told the coroner that no doubt, a major mistake had been made on the part of her husband as she had never once set foot on a stage. It had been a tragic case of misrecognition.

18. A Drive along the Mersey

Through a painfully ironic twist of fate, forty-year-old car salesman John Wilson became the victim of a dreadful motor calamity back in the year 1913. On the Saturday afternoon of 1 March John arranged to a meet an acquaintance by the name of Florence Phillips at the Liverpool Landing Stage. He carefully navigated his car through the busy roads of the city before pulling up alongside the Liver Building to meet his awaiting companion. He was by all accounts an expert driver, having driven almost every type of car through his employment at the Rodney Street showroom of J. Blake & Co. After exchanging pleasantries with Mrs Phillips John started up the engine, drove over to the pier and up onto the deck of a Birkenhead-bound steamer. The pair were heading over to Cheshire and through to the Welsh town of Llangollen where Mr Wilson had a business meeting to attend. The outward drive through the tranquil countryside proved largely uneventful but it was their return trip that was to result in terribly tragic consequences. That evening the couple arrived back at Woodside and, just as before, John drove the car onto the boat positioning it safely on the deck facing the Wirral shore. He put on the handbrake and killed the engine. With all passengers happily on board the order was given to depart and the vessel started its smooth sail out into the river. On nearing Liverpool Mr Wilson heaved himself up into the driving seat of his motor car and prepared to depart. Florence watched as he revved up the engine and pressed down a large button with his foot. This sent the car jolting forwards and the two front wheels began to skid uncontrollably, lifting off the ground. A huge cry followed as Mr Wilson was sent crashing through the steamer's wooden barrier and off overboard into the cold waters of the Mersey. Two passengers, Michael Hughes and David Jones, were unlucky enough to be knocked off balance and fell with Mr Wilson down into the water as the vessel lay approximately 100 yards from shore. Life buoys were flung down to the men and quick-thinking ferry master Samuel Partington despatched the steamer's lifeboat on an urgent rescue mission. Both Hughes and Jones were saved but despite the most earnest attempts at revival, John Wilson sadly perished in the accident. His body, once recovered from the water, was examined by doctors. They found it to exhibit only minor abrasions, strongly suggesting that Wilson died from drowning and not from injuries he received during the crash. At an inquest the following week a jury accepted that John had most likely left his vehicle in gear and upon starting the engine, had mistakenly put the car into fatal motion. They returned a verdict of 'accidently drowned'.

The Liverpool Landing Stage where the car and its driver plummeted into the river.

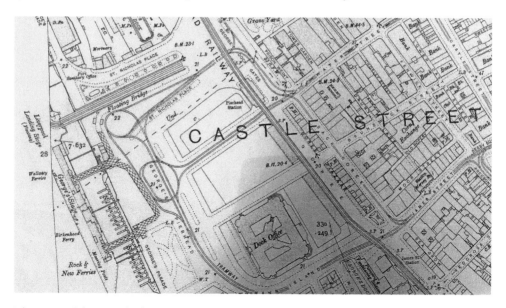

The scene of the tragedy shown at the turn of the twentieth century.

19. The Lunatic of Rainhill

By the turn of the twentieth century, twenty-nine-year-old Mary Grainger had already been an inmate of three different mental institutions, suffering from rigorous episodes of depression and paranoia. In March 1900 she was removed from the Toxteth Workhouse and placed under the supervision of staff at Rainhill Lunatic Asylum. Mary's progress appeared most favourable and she was seen to be practically convalescent by attendants closest to her. On 1 August at around 8.30 a.m. Mary was carrying out some domestic work for the superintendent Dr Wigglesworth along with fellow patient Hannah Hancox, a former tailoress. For a short while the pair where left alone unsupervised to clean and tidy when suddenly the silence of the asylum was broken by terrific screams for mercy. Dr Wigglesworth came running into the room and found Hannah down on the floor with blood spewing out from the pierced veins of her neck. Above her sat Mary Grainger and in her grasp she held a small breadknife stolen from the matron's kitchen. Hannah's head lay to one side as Mary sawed away with great violence only relinquishing her fury when dragged physically to the floor and restrained by mortified asylum attendants. Dr Wigglesworth set about stemming the flow from Hannah's deeply mutilated oesophagus but with so much blood already amassed upon the floor, death was the only outcome. Mary stated quite coherently that upon waking that morning

Reeve Court retirement village now occupies the site of the lunatic asylum.

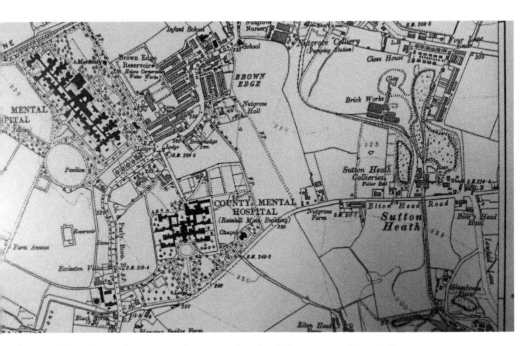

The Rainhill Asylum where Hannah Hancox lost her life, seen on a historical map.

she felt an irresistible urge to kill, to kill anybody. It was pure misfortunate that her victim was the forty-nine-year-old Hannah and her murderous mental relapse was a shock to all.

Later that week Mary stood trial before magistrates but it appeared to her that she was assisting in some sort of marriage ceremony, singing, whistling and asking bizarre questions to all present. The young woman was clearly insane but for a crime such as murder she would have no choice but to stand trial before a Crown Court and face the highest of penalties. News of the grisly affair reached the office of the Home Secretary Sir Matthew White Ridley who ordered a halt to the proceedings and he had Mary admitted to Broadmoor. She was to be officially locked away for fear of public safety allowed only to reside with the criminally insane for the rest of her days.

20. An Accidental Shot

At around 9.30 p.m. on a Saturday in July 1832, Mrs Foster, the wife of a town policeman, returned to her Cumberland Street home. Before then she had left the house in the hands of her good friend Mary Hampton, who had come to visit along with her granddaughter. Upon her return Mrs Hampton excitedly grabbed Mary and was quick to warn her of an unwanted visitor sneaking about the rooms. The woman's heart skipped a beat but this was no human assailant. A cat, one which had shrewdly crept into the house was now prowling about upstairs bedrooms after trying to claw open the family's birdcage. Mary confessed that she had been too afraid to approach and her efforts to shoo the cat away proved pointless. Mrs Foster told her friend not to worry; the problem would soon be dealt with. She walked over to the fireplace and from above brought down one of her husband's pistols which had hung decoratively on the wall. With the weapon in hand Mrs Foster led the way and all three females headed up the staircase on the hunt for the invasive feline. It was not long that through some peculiar accident, it was to be Mrs Hampton who became victim to the gun's speeding contents and she fell down dead in an instant. It was said Mrs Foster had been somewhat intoxicated at the time and did not realise what she had done until some moments later. No doubt the horror of bringing an end to the life of her closest friend was a deeply sobering sensation. The coroner's investigation the following week believed the affair to be entirely accidental and a jury returned a verdict to that effect.

Cumberland Street where the accidental shot was fired.

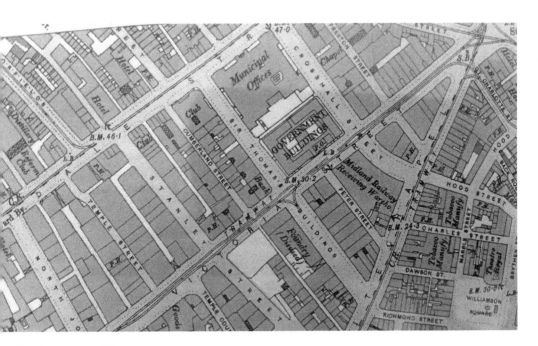

The site of the incident seen on a contemporary map.

21. Death at a Funeral

On the wet afternoon of 3 June 1896 a sombre crowd descended upon Anfield Cemetery. That Wednesday was the day of the funeral of the elderly Susan McFarlane, the former resident of Red House in Upton, Wirral. Her body lay solemnly in a wooden casket surrounded by tearful friends and family members who had all come to pay their final and everlasting respects.

Among them was undertaker John Howson Smith from the Birkenhead firm Messrs Higgins & Smith. He was stood at the graveside gently lowering the coffin into the ground with the assistance of his black-attired colleagues gripping the ropes tightly, allowing the box to descend deep into the freshly dug grave. All of a sudden Smith became rather ill. He felt breathless and his hands began to shake forcing his imperative grasp on the rope to be relinquished. This act sent the coffin down at an angle slamming into the soil as horrified gasps cried out from tearful well-wishers. Smith himself collapsed and lunged back towards a headstone for support. 'Water!' he wheezed, holding onto the monument. 'I need a drink of water.' Mr Hogg and

Anfield Cemetery where John H. Smith took his final breath.

Mr Abbot, his fellow undertakers, hurried over to the forty-three-year-old and helped him to a seat. After a much-needed drink and on recovering his composure Smith uttered that he had the strangest sensation that he had been sleeping, and how before he knew what was happening, he was on the ground. He said that he expected to be alright but would remain seated for the time being.

The funeral was soon back underway and the remaining undertakers stood silently, heads bowed as the clergyman quoted the appropriate verses. A few moments of quiet grief passed before, once again, the undertaker Smith caused a commotion among the mourners.

'In the midst of life we are death' preached the vicar and with those words, Smith's head fell back and a vacant gaze fell across his face. The woeful crowd were at a loss to what had happened. Attempts were made to rouse the man from his cadaver-like state but with no response, Smith was placed into the back of the nearest vehicle, a mourning brougham, and taken to a doctor. On arrival it was found that no medicine could possibly save him now. Smith had died at the funeral.

An inquest was held the following day before the city coroner and it was heard how, on the afternoon of the funeral, the deceased had been caught in a shower of rain and to avoid getting wet had run rather too quickly to the cemetery office. It was believed this exertion, along with his already debilitating muscular rheumatism ultimately led to his premature end. He left a widow and several children. A verdict of death from natural causes was returned.

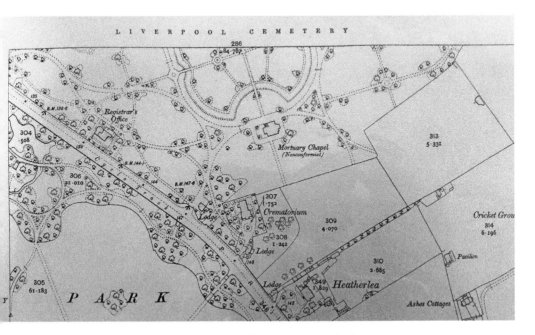

Anfield Cemetery was the setting of the undertaker's own untimely demise.

22. A Terminal Teapot

The remains of Shaw Hill Street, seen in modern times.

On Tuesday 6 November 1832, Catherine Parry of Shawhill Street came to the Coroner's Court to give evidence surrounding the untimely death of her young son Stephen. She spoke tearfully about the tragic events of the previous Friday afternoon when she was in the act of pouring a cup of tea. Stephen was standing very near to her directly under the pot, no doubt seeking his mother's attention. Tragedy struck when the container suddenly crackled and a piece of ceramic fell from its base. A cascade of blistering water followed, raining down upon the boy and scalding him dreadfully upon his head and upper body. Mrs Parry immediately ran with the crying toddler to the dispensary where a surgeon assessed the damage. Medics attempted to keep the boy alive as best as they could, but his burns were so severe his short life ended just 48 hours later. A verdict of accidental death was declared.

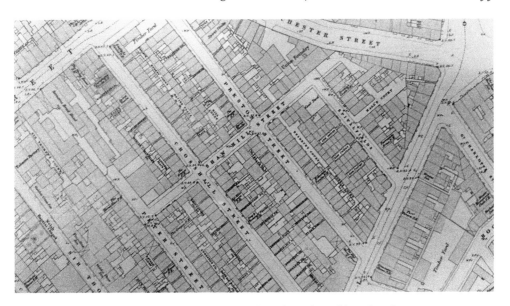

In the Victorian-era Shawhill Street was a typical residential neighbourhood.

23. Ungracious in Defeat

On Friday 16 December 1864, Judge Mellor presided over a piercing matter involving two jobbing gardeners at Liverpool Crown Court. Thirty-year-old Felix O'Hare stood charged with causing the death of his former friend, Patrick Fleming. It was heard how on the Saturday evening of 10 September the two men were drinking at Rae's public house on the corner of Lawson Street and Melville Place, where they became steadily intoxicated. The labourers laid their particularly ghoulish tools of their trade, a pair of scythes, at the back door while they sat, drank and played cards; the loser was to the pay for the beer. As the night drew on O'Hare's luck began to run out and it seemed certain that he would be forced to cough up the dough and buy the booze. 'If you don't pay for the ale I'll cut the eyes out of your head!' the Irishman threatened unexpectedly, then landing a solid punch to Fleming's face. This caused his nose to well-up with blood and eye to blacken. The elder man seemed somewhat stunned by the assault. He stepped away from the table and without saying a word walked to the backyard to clean his wound. O'Hare followed him out and grabbed his scythe. 'I'll cut you in two if you don't pay for the ale,' bawled the drunkard. He took aim and he swung his menacing tool down hard into Fleming's leg. The blade penetrated deep into the left thigh, causing a gaping fleshy hole. Bleeding and in shock, Fleming rushed back into the pub and called out to his friend James Vennard, 'Jimmy, I must go as quick as

I can to the hospital!' The fifty-eight-year-old left the pub and hobbled down the street towards the infirmary. A passer-by saw him struggling and helped him on his way.

At the hospital the injured gardener was seen by Dr Nash and Dr Bickersteth. They observed that Fleming was sporting a very dangerous wound running approximately 5 inches down to the bone, and bacterial infection was beginning to take hold. Detective Cousens and Constable Bainbridge began a search for the assailant who they found in bed at a court dwelling near Elm Grove. He was arrested and placed in the cells, all the while protesting his innocence. O'Hare insisted that that Fleming had fallen on his scythe while drunk, and that is how he came by the injury. From his hospital bed Fleming's condition was worsening and hope of a recovery was minute. Almost two weeks after being admitted, Patrick Fleming passed away. Under Judge Mellor's direction, the question for the jury was to decide whether this was a case of murder or manslaughter. After a short absence the twelve members returned to the room and announced their verdict. They determined the prisoner guilty of manslaughter and O'Hare was sentenced to ten years penal servitude.

Mellville Place, where the deadly attack occurred.

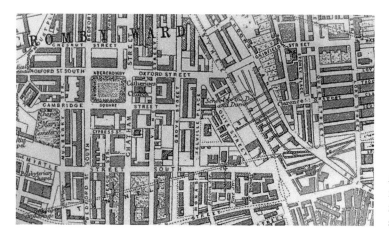

A late nineteenth-century map shows the scene of the crime.

24. Hardcore Partying

The former location of Embledon Terrace. No trace of the original property remains.

Nineteen-year-old Ellen Roberts had set off from her Edge Hill home to her friend's house in Embledon Terrace to partake in a night of birthday celebrations. On arrival the teenage housemaid appeared very well and in very cheerful spirits. Shortly before 10.00 p.m. she was seen to ask another female partygoer for a waltz around the kitchen. This offer was happily accepted and the evening's events were turning out to be very pleasant indeed. On ending a dance for a second time, Ellen suddenly collapsed and fell backwards against a sofa in a state of exhaustion, but something was seriously wrong. The mood of the party took a turn for the worse when it was found Ellen was out cold. An ambulance was called and the girl taken to the Royal Southern Hospital for emergency treatment. Doctors however failed to find a pulse. She was dead. A medical investigation discovered two blood vessels at the base of Miss Robert's brain had given way, creating the pressure that had been the cause of her demise. This, doctors believed, had been brought about by her laborious dance moves earlier that evening. An inquest held on 25 April 1906 returned a verdict of natural causes.

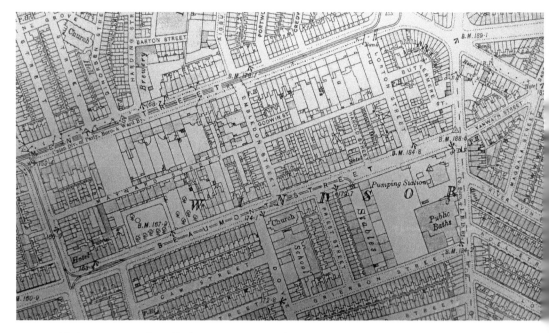

Embledon Terrace, off Embledon Street, was the location of the ill-fated party.

25. The Suspicions of Mr Leonard

Owen Leonard was a tailor's assistant in his early sixties. He and his wife Bridget lived at No. 37 Peter Street in Liverpool's Whitechapel district, along with their family and an assortment of lodgers. The layout was simple: at the top of the building lodged the lodgers, on the second floor lived the Leonards and on the ground floor was a kitchen and living area. Living together happily however was not so straightforward. Of late Owen had become somewhat suspicious of Bridget and believed that she was having an affair with one of their recent tenants. It was a deeply suspicious notion that was sending the aged man to his wits' end. On the night of 27 July 1844, Owen, Bridget, tenants Mr and Mrs Livingston and an unnamed male lodger were sitting together in the kitchen in the warm glow of a burning fireplace. They talked and chatted politely enough, but it was this man who Owen suspected of making certain advances towards his wife. He bit his lip but it was only minutes before the elderly man's patience finally ran out and he could no longer keep up his calm pretence. His anger reached boiling point and he had had a drop to drink, Dutch courage, but he knew perfectly well what he was doing. Alcohol and rage flowed in Owens's veins as he stood up to seemingly tower over the startled house guest. He ordered the lodger to pack up and leave at once; he was no longer welcome at the house and could not stay another minute. The surprised individual initially refused stating that it was far too late for him to go now, and John Livingston agreed. 'It's a bit unfair to turn him out at this hour, after all he has paid for his lodging as well,' he said. These niceties fell upon death ears as the furious landlord held onto the man forcefully by collar, knuckles white, and continued to seethe his demands for a swift exit. A worried Bridget implored him to go. 'Please leave, or there shall be a row,' she begged. Mrs Leonard rushed to collect the now ex-tenant's rent money that he had paid and returned it to him. She shoved the money in his hands as hers shook with fret. The unwanted visitor put on his coat and left, never to be seen again. Owen had followed the man out into the darkness of the street, making sure he had left for good when neighbour Henry Jones came walking home. He turned the corner into Peter Street at about half-past twelve from where he spotted Mr Leonard pacing the ground outside his house. He seemed very much agitated, with Mrs Leonard following closely behind. She was muttering things in a low, hushed voice trying to get her husband to listen. Henry thought nothing of it and went into his own house opposite the Leonards' and headed upstairs for a good night's sleep.

In the cool fresh air Owens's temper began to wane but he still held a deep mistrust of his wife. Both parties returned indoors where Owen locked the door and shut the windows. In the meantime Bridget had escorted Mr and Mrs Livingston up the dark staircase to their room with the guidance of a small flickering candle. Her hand continued to shake ever so slightly due to the drama that had taken place, but once upstairs the woman gradually regained her normally resolute composure and spoke happily with the couple for around ten minutes. Then Owen appeared. 'I'd like to see you downstairs,' he told her, with an unusual tone of haste. He then left without saying another word. Bridget sighed and bid the Livingstons a good night before following her husband down to the lower floors of the house. Owen had a bone to pick, calling her a bitch and a whore for her supposed adultery. 'Aye sure. Yes sure,' Bridget answered indifferently, refusing to engage in any arguments so late at night. Their fourteen-year-old son James was still awake and could hear the domestic altercation from the second floor. Mrs Leonard sighed and headed upstairs to fetch a blanket and returned downstairs to be greeted with more marital aggression. James had followed her down and he witnessed his parents arguing over a man called John Guest, who in Owen's mind the sexagenarian Bridget had also had relations with. 'Aye sure. Yes sure,' she repeated before attempting to strike her accuser with a slap into reality. This indifference sent Owen to the brink. He raised his fist and sent Bridget flying down from her seat onto the solid cold floor. She fell back against the kitchen door and fell to the ground screaming in fear. Like a green-eyed deranged beast Owen seized Bridget by the neck and withdrew a blade from his pocket. He brandished the razor tight within his furious fist and inflicted his hate. Bridget was soon suffering from a slice across her throat which began to gush forth with blood. 'Murder! Murder!' Young James had seen it all and called out in horror. Owen turned and stared at the boy with a savage and sinister stare and shook his head in a slow unnerving manner. James quickly ran from the kitchen as the screams of his mother continued to echo about the house.

The tower of the Municipal Buildings now overlooks Peter Street.

Michel Hamilton lived nearby and was awoken by the mayhem. He quickly got dressed and barged into the house towards the cries for help. He attempted to open the kitchen door but couldn't. It was stuck. Bridget was lying against it and Owen was standing over her carrying out an inhuman and malevolent attack. The door then slammed into Mr Hamilton's face knocking him back in a daze. On his second try the hawker managed to force the door open slightly and saw Mr Leonard make a stab at the old woman with his razor. 'You old villain!' He shouted, with a mix of dread and anger, 'what are you doing to your wife?' There was no response, only screams for mercy.

Margaret Peacock also lived in Peter Street and was a good friend of the Leonards. She too had heard the cries and went across soon after Michel Hamilton. She was there when the kitchen door was finally forced open and Bridget was found lying on the tiles in a pool of her own blood. 'Keep him in!' pleaded Mrs Leonard. She was adamant that her husband would not run to escape his fate. She repeated this three times while calling for a policeman. With her strength sapping in lethal measures, Bridget gestured towards Mrs Peacock with a weak hand and begged for help: 'Put something to me or I shall die, for he has cut my throat.' She took off her apron and pressed it hard against the woman's bleeding gullet. 'You bloody murderer!' Margaret cried, as Owen looked on proudly. He threatened to do the same to her but thankfully refrained from any more murderous pandemonium. He remained in the kitchen as neighbours carried Bridget out into the street. Owen locked the door behind them.

'Oh policeman, do come here! My father is murdering my mother!' PC Dunn had been walking his beat along Sir Thomas Street when Master Leonard ran up to him panic-stricken and incredibly alarmed. He had managed to unbolt the door and run for help. The two figures ran to Peter Street where they found Bridget lying on the pavement surrounded by neighbours. She had managed to be rescued from Owen but had sustained some truly horrific wounds. She was missing the tip of her nose and now exhibited only a stump of bleeding nasal tissue, her neck featured a pair of large razorblade cuts and her blood count was deteriorating rapidly. PC Burns ran to the scene after hearing the commotion and he and PC Dunn headed to the front door, but it was locked. With great gusto they forced it down and moved on in. In the kitchen stood Owen Leonard wiping his bloodstained hands with a cloth. His clothes bore witness to the carnage he had inflicted: his pants dripping with Bridget's blood. 'Why have you done this?' asked an officer. 'She's an old bitch' he shrugged, and that was all he said. Constable Dunn promptly arrested Mr Leonard and locked him up, and Constable Burns retrieved the bloody razor lying open on the kitchen floor. Samuel Potter, a surgeon was called and he arrived on the scene at about two o'clock. He speedily dressed the old woman's wounds and had her sent to the Northern Hospital. His prognosis was miserably pessimistic and as expected Bridget passed away from her wounds. She was dead on arrival.

Coroner Curry held an inquest the next day where a full investigation into Mrs Leonard's death took place before a jury of the most respectable tradesman of Lord Street. They had viewed the mutilated body and now sat in an inquest room waiting to hear the grisly circumstances of the case. Owen was brought into the

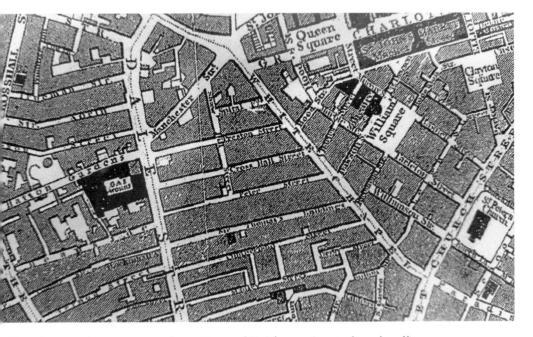

Peter Street as shown on a map from 1841, and Sir Thomas Street where the officer was summoned.

room, standing at about five feet four inches with a very slender frame, and the inquest began. James Leonard, the killer's teenage son was first to give evidence and told the court his version of events. He confirmed that the razor shown to the jury was the very same weapon that had inflicted the appalling wounds upon his mother. Police officers Dunn and Burns related their accounts, as did John Livingston, Michael Hamilton, Margaret Peacock and Samuel Potter. Edward Parker, house surgeon from the Northern Hospital, informed the coroner of the result of his intricately conducted post-mortem. His findings showed that Mrs Leonard's injuries were quite numerous. She had wound on the left check: an incision extending from the upper lip across the left check to the ear, approximately five inches in length and three quarters in depth, and which divided the arteries. There were two more slight wounds on the left side of the victim's neck and a transverse slice, around four inches in length and one inch deep which divided the jugular. There was more: another wound on her neck was found extending down to the windpipe and it divided several muscles in the front of the neck; a slice on the back of the woman's left forearm extended obliquely towards the elbow and exposed and partly divided her arm muscles; further down towards the legs there was a deep laceration on the left thigh; and a wound on her left knee about three inches deep down to the bone and it separated a large vein and artery of considerable size. Dr Parker judged the wounds to have all been caused by a sharp instrument, a razor most probably, and death was caused by haemorrhage from the abundance of wounds on the whole rather than one single injury.

Owen Leonard was cautioned in the usual way and asked if he had anything to say. 'Nothing at present' was his blasé reply.

The jury immediately returned a verdict of wilful murder and under the coroner's warrant the prisoner was committed to the assizes. The verdict seemed to have no outward effect upon Mr Leonard, but a short consultation with his two daughters Ann and Margaret, and his son James, transformed his demeanour to one of great sadness.

Officers removed Owen to a Kirkdale Gaol cell to await his trial and on 26 August Owen Leonard faced the judge and jury of the court where the facts of the case were reiterated. New witnesses called included Thomas Chalmer, the surgeon of Kirkdale Gaol who had observed the prisoner's behaviour. It was his belief that Mr Leonard was not suffering from insanity nor showed any symptoms of a diseased mind: 'He appears to be perfectly conscious of what is going on and I believe is a sound-minded individual.' On cross-examination Dr Chalmer replied that he had gained his in-depth knowledge on the subject from experience and through reading various works. 'Hardly an assize takes place in which I am not called upon to give my opinion on the question of insanity,' explained the learned physician.

Mr McAubrey was placed for the defence. He addressed the jury on behalf of Mr Leonard and argued that the act undoubtedly committed by his client could not be considered as murder, or even manslaughter. 'Every circumstance in this case shows there was neither reason nor design,' the jury heard. 'It has been shown in the evidence that the deceased struck first, and no doubt the prisoner, in the heat of passion put his hand in his pocket and commenced the senseless and irrational cutting and slashing.' Mr McAubrey continued and pledged to show that Owen Leonard had changed from a previously quiet and peaceful man to ungovernable and vicious, exhibiting every symptom of an abbreviation of intellect. He called Margaret Leonard to the stand.

'My father was some years ago a mild, kind, gentle and religious man behaving well to his family. About five years ago he became suddenly changed, his conversation altered and his manner also; he spoke indifferently to my mother, composed poems and songs, and, for a trifle, he would strike anyone who came near him.'

Mr McAubery nodded as he listened, and asked the witness to further give further evidence in regards to his client's warped state of mind.

'He fancied mother would poison him and would not take tea until someone tasted it first,' Margaret answered.

Ann Leonard was also questioned. She recalled a time around a month before the incident when she had been at the Peter Street house and her father had asked her for some money. She had none with her, but on hearing this Owen threw her brother James across the room in a blind temper and struck her, screaming that she was not his daughter and accused her mother of infidelity without cause. 'I had a very great fear of him,' she muttered meekly.

A similar testimony was given by John Goodwin, Mr Leonard's employer. He lived in the Sir Thomas Buildings and made a living as a master tailor. He told the court that he had known the prisoner for a very long time, nearly thirty years, and that he had used to be a quiet, inoffensive man but for the last four years or so had noticed Owen to become very irritable without any reason and that he had a tendency to ramble. 'Sometimes, when I gave him orders he darted rapidly out of the building,' said Mr Goodwin. He considered Owen to be at times insane in his ways.

There was still room for a counterargument. Mr Hulton for the prosecution argued that if Owen Leonard was guilty then it was to the full extent of the indictment. 'All of the facts of the case show premeditation and even the evidence for the prosecution have been corroborated in great measure by witnesses for the defence.' He addressed the jury and pressed them to believe that the prisoner was a responsible being at the time of the offence, and if, as suggested, Owen had been intoxicated then he was still accountable for his deadly actions.

There was no other conclusion than to say that Bridget had died from the wounds inflicted upon her by her husband. The question for the jury to decide was whether the prisoner standing before them was responsible and accountable at the time of the killing. Was Mr Leonard acting on motive, knowing what he was doing, or was he in such a deranged mental state arising from some unknown psychological disease, not intemperance, as to not be in control of his awful actions that terrible morning in July?

There was much deliberation but a verdict was finally given by the foreman. The learned gentlemen of the jury had decided and found the prisoner to be guilty of the crime of manslaughter. For this, Owen Leonard was sentenced to transportation for life.

26. A Deadly Exchange

The Exchange Flags where the fatal accident took place, photographed in the early twentieth century.

In November 1816, a most miserable accident occurred to pub landlady Mrs Oaks as she walked across the cobbles of Exchange Square. On the afternoon of the 12th a gang of workmen had been employed to carry out some building work on one portion of the Exchange. They were in process of hoisting a heavy beam through an open window by means of a rope when Mrs Oakes neared the gate to the public office. This was directly beneath the foreboding, wavering beam and by some dreadful chance, it was at this precise moment that the beam slipped free from its support and crashed down in an oblique descent right on top of her. Mrs Oaks herself then fell to the ground amid a torrent of her own blood, dying almost immediately. She had been the owner of a tavern near St Paul's Square, only moments away from the scene.

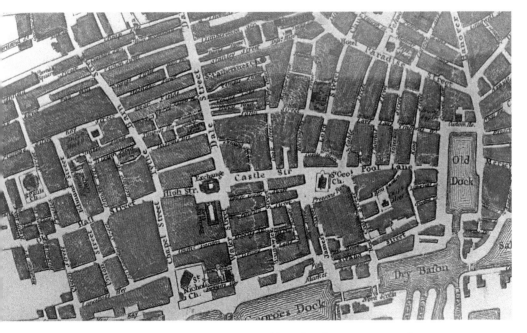

An early view of the Exchange and surrounding neighbourhood, seen on a map from 1795.

27. The Rat's Banquet

On Tuesday 1 June 1858, an inquest was held into the passing of forty-nine-year-old Mary Hammond. She had been the wife of Robert, a grocer's assistant and the pair had lived in a modest property in Pownall Square. The details of the inquest revealed that Mary had been in a rather depressed state of mind in the weeks leading up to her death and could be often found drinking at intermittent times of the day. This may have been the result of a nasty accident which saw the middle-aged woman plummet down a flight of stairs. She, however, never complained of any lasting pain from the mishap, but little could be done to raise her melancholy spirits. On the evening of Sunday 30 May, it was heard that Mary had told her husband she would be staying in the parlour that night to sleep on the sofa. On rising the following morning Robert found to his dismay that his wife had died in her sleep. To add to the poor man's horror, rats had been the first to discover his bereavement and in the dead of night, eaten away Mrs Hammond's eyes and a large portion of her upper lip. A verdict of natural causes was returned.

Pownall Square, where a family of rats feasted on Mrs Hammond's remains.

A contemporary map depicts the scene of the monstrous events.

28. Dangerous Weather

The year 1832 brought some particularly dreadful weather to the region and with it, mortal chaos. The streets were battered by torrents of rain and showers of giant hailstones, some of which were so huge many green-fingered locals feared for the crops in their gardens and the fruit in their orchards. On Tuesday 12 June a great storm erupted, lasting nearly the whole of the day and flooding the areas of Paradise Street and Whitechapel to a depth of nearly 3 feet. The wise-thinking shopkeepers in the area had heeded warnings of the weather, but the poor cellar dwellers had little defence and suffered both in health and property. There too came severe bouts of lightening which caused notable damage to the premises of Mr Jones, a tanner in Marybone. Many others saw the destruction of their windows and shards of glass had to be avoided on many water-logged pavements. During one incident a streak of lightning struck the eleven-year-old daughter of Mrs Bryson. The girl was first rendered blind through the calamity and later perished from terrible internal injuries. More fatalities occurred in the city outskirts. Several servants employed by Mrs Leyland of Walton Hall were in the middle of cutting through thistles in nearby land when dark clouds gathered overhead. Foolishly, the lodge-keeper and a fellow servant ran to take shelter under a tree, taking their long metal scythes in hand. The lodge-keeper was stuck dead immediately as electricity passed through his body like a wire and little hope was given to his companion, who it was thought was unlikely to ever recover from his own unconscious state.

The vast and verdant grounds of Walton Hall have since become a public park.

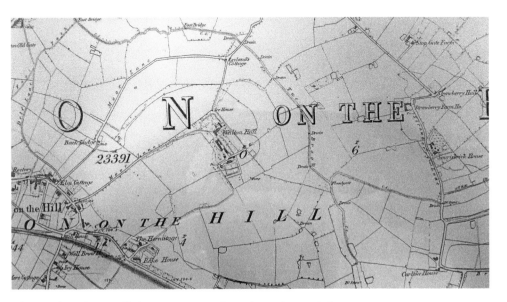

The stately Walton Hall shown on a map from the mid-twentieth century.

29. A Waking Nightmare

The original site of Nesfield Street has since disappeared from the cityscape.

In February 1906 the city coroner held an inquiry into the strange circumstances surrounding the death of Thomas Woof. The twenty-nine-year-old had been, like many Liverpudlians, a dock labourer and lived in a simple house in Anfield's Nesfield Street. On 27 January Thomas felt tired and went upstairs for a lie down. Around thirty minutes had passed when his wife suddenly heard a succession of noises becoming louder and louder with every thump. She hastily made her way out into the hallway and to her shock discovered Thomas lying at the foot of the stairs in an astonished state. Fortunately he was still conscious and so could explain the origin of his inadvertent fall. Thomas remarked how he had fallen asleep and had begun to experience a very lucid dream. He had dreamt that he had been going for some coal to put on the kitchen fire and had opened the bedroom door, thinking it was the coal place. On walking out he was jolted from his slumber and was tumbling downstairs at a white-knuckle pace. The fall had been quite a dangerous one so Thomas was taken to the Stanley Hospital as a precautionary measure. This proved to be a most sensible move as his condition worsened considerably. Unfortunately doctors were unable to save him and his passing was officially recorded as a terrible accident.

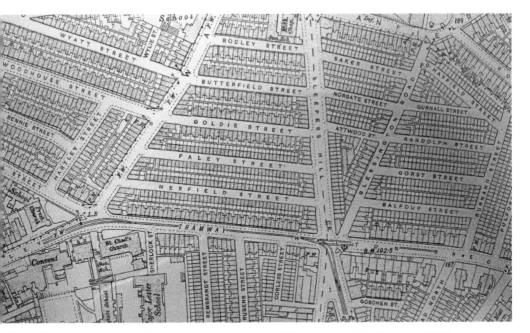

Nesfield Street was originally located near to Sleepers Hill, between Faley Street and Walton Breck Road.

30. Man on Fire

On the night of Saturday 13 March 1869, Mary Ann Crawley ran into Matthew Woodlock's coal yard in a terrible state. His family were coal dealers living in Almond Street near to Mrs Crawley's house and he was very surprised to see her in such a hysterical state. 'Why are you here to make rows?' asked Matthew in his confusion. The woman gave no answer but barged her way past in a frantic fright. Matthew went to the door of the yard and looked out to see what Mary was so afraid of. To his amazement Mr Woodlock noticed that a small crowd had gathered and there were a number of inquisitive faces peering out from the windows. His eyes squinted and he scanned the urban vista for the mysterious late-night attraction. Just then a burning, screaming silhouette ran from Mary's house five doors down and roared past him towards a moonlit Crown Street. A man was on fire and jets of flames spread out from his waving arms and legs. 'Help! Help!' he cried as terrified onlookers stood aghast in dumbstruck horror. The man fell to his knees, then face first into the ground as neighbour James Corless rushed forth and courageously patted out the flames with his recently purchased overcoat. A second man assisted in this brave and noble act and soon enough the flames were successfully extinguished. 'It was in a row,' uttered Mary,

The neighbourhood has since been redeveloped for the Liverpool Women's Hospital.

'the oil got on the fire and from that to him.' She and Mr Woodlock ventured out into the street which was becoming abuzz with a mass of interested locals. 'Who was that man?' asked Elizabeth Hughes, a butcher's wife from further down the road. 'Why it's Crawley of course,' spat Mary, the man's wife, 'let him be burned. To the Devil with him!' Constable William Walls was on the scene in a matter of moments and had Mr Crawley conveyed to the Royal Infirmary for doctors to assess his condition. It was unknown whether the man would survive the night. Constable Wells returned to the scene, arrested Mrs Crawley and charged her with throwing oil at her husband. 'He struck me with his fist!' she sobbed, 'he threw a plate and struck me at the back of my head, and pulled my hair.' Mary was remanded in the cells until she could be seen by a magistrate and plead her case. On Monday 15 March, Detective Marsden paid a visit to her house at No. 1 Lonsdale Road. On stepping into the kitchen, the sleuth detected a quantity of paraffin had splashed across the hearth and mantelpiece. Lying under the fire grate were several large fragments of glass. Detective Marsden carefully bent down and retrieved the biggest piece and placed it under his discerning nostrils, 'paraffin oil.'

On Tuesday 23 March Mrs Crawley was brought before Mr Raffles for trial. Her charge now was one of manslaughter. Her husband of fourteen years had died two days previously. Several witnesses including the deceased's brother, Elizabeth Hughes, James Corless, PC Wells and Detective Marsden gave evidence, as well as Dr George Orton from the Royal Infirmary. Upon taking the stand Dr Orton stated how Mr Crawley had been brought into his ward on the night of the 13th suffering from severe burns. The whole of his head was scorched with his left arm burnt all over: right from the tips of his fingers to the top of his shoulder. His right arm and back were also terribly burnt and Mr Crawley had also lost his beard and moustache in the facial inferno. However,

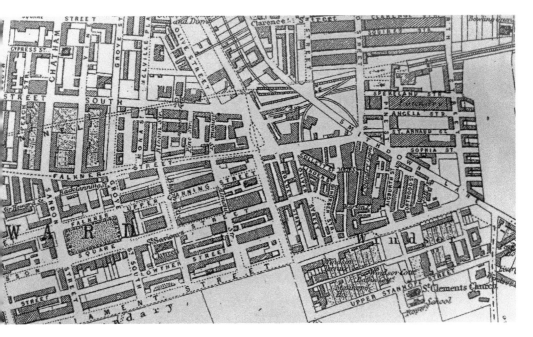

Lonsdale Street was a continuation of Lowther Street, as seen on this late nineteenth-century map.

death was due to a state of lockjaw caused by the burns. The doctor stated that his passing took place at 2.30 p.m. on Sunday. Before his death Michel was able to give a statement and affix his mark. This was read out to the court:

> I came home a little intoxicated. I wanted to go out, and I asked my wife to go and bring some things we had in pledge. She refused to do so, and I hit her with my fist on her head with my left hand. She turned round. There was a bottle of paraffin oil on the table and she threw it at me unawares. I mean, my back was towards her, and I did not know she was going to do it or I should have stopped her. I found myself all in a blaze. I ran out into the street.

Mrs Crawley was asked whether she wished to say anything further before Mr Raffles made his decision. 'I am very sorry but I never threw the oil to burn him. I know nothing of how it caught fire,' she answered. Mr Raffles ordered the prisoner to be sent on to the Crown Court on the charge of manslaughter. It was there on 31 March where she stood before Justice Lush.

The evidence of the magistrates' court was repeated, including the inspection of the broken paraffin bottle and the charred clothing that the deceased was wearing on the night in question. Mr Hawthorne for the defence contended that Mary became scared after being punched by Mr Crawley and fearing further blows, took up the first thing she could lay her hands upon to protect herself – the paraffin container. If the bottle was indeed thrown, as the evidence suggested, at the deceased with his back towards the fireplace, the smashing of the container and the spilling of its contents was probable cause for his clothes igniting and the subsequent blaze.

Judge Lush mused over the details, as did the assembled jury who soon found Mary guilty of the charge of manslaughter but issued her with a strong recommendation for mercy. This was duly granted and a one day spell of imprisonment was handed down to the prisoner who felt great relief at the forgiving outcome.

31. Aeronautical Delusions

On 23 September 1914 the Liverpool Coroner held an inquest examining the unusual circumstances of the death of Florence Bloore. The fifty-two-year-old was said to have suffered from a series of incredible delusions and was under the impression that everyone was persecuting her. Mrs Bloore had even complained to the authorities that a gentleman had flown over her house in Lime Grove in an aeroplane and verbally threatened her down the chimney. She claimed Harold Gill of Parkgate had shouted at her from his plane as he flew overhead and had threatened to cut her up. She had sent threatening letters to Mr Gill in retaliation, much to his annoyance and to the dismay of the young man's parents. For this she had been fined 2 guineas in costs and ordered to cease her wild accusations. So obsessed was she with this idea that the woman would cry out at night that the man in an aeroplane was after her and no one could convince her otherwise. Following her unsuccessful court action Florence ended it all by taking poison, and a sad verdict of suicide while of unsound mind was returned.

Lime Grove, the scene of Florence Bloore's bizarre allegations and subsequent death.

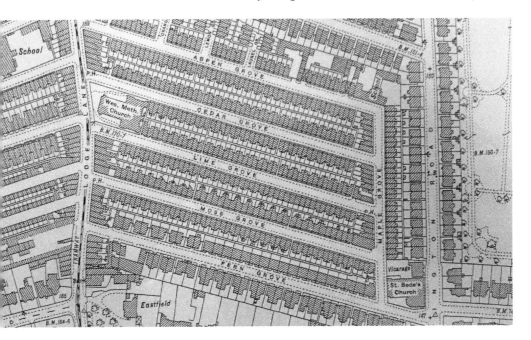

A map showing where Florence Bloore resided in Lime Grove, close to Lodge Lane.

32. The Heavy Weight

A rather macabre case occurred on the night of 10 August 1903, when Mrs Shortis of Oakes Street perished through very bizarre circumstances. That night, the aged Mr Shortis and his wife had headed upstairs to retire for the evening. Tragically Mrs Shortis missed her footing and suddenly slipped backwards onto her partner. The force sent them both plummeting down the stairs where the elderly woman sustained a broken neck, dying that instant. She was by no means a petite lady, weighing approximately 17 stone. Her heavy and lifeless body lay on top of her husband who could summon no energy to free himself from this gruesome embrace. Four days passed before their daughter called at the house to check up on her parents. On receiving no answer to her repeated knocks a constable was summoned to investigate. He entered the property through a cellar window and was shocked to discover the unpleasant scene within. He found the old man alive but in a serious state of exhaustion beneath the decomposing frame of his dearly beloved. Mr Shortis could hardly breathe as the cold cadaver of his wife weighed down heavy upon his ever-weakening bones. On finally being rescued from this horrific situation, little hope was given of recovery and he himself perished the following morning at the Liverpool Workhouse.

Oakes Street, where Mr and Mrs Shortis resided, shown in modern times.

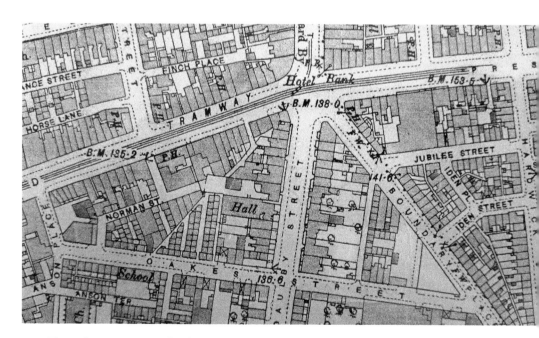

The unfortunate setting for the gruesome affair, seen on a twentieth-century map.

33. A Bird without Wings

On 7 July 1865 an unfortunate few witnessed the tragic death of the Liverpool barrister William Bird. Mr Bird lived at Ivy House, Aigburth but on the night in question was a guest of the Alexandra Hotel in Dale Street. That evening he had met up with his friend Mr Hughes and a gathering of mutual acquaintances for dinner and chit-chat. After eating, most of the party left to go to the theatre leaving Mr Hughes and Mr Bird to a night of carefree drinking and banter. By 11.00 p.m. the intoxicated lawman was feeling rather worse for wear so settled down in a seat by the window on the first floor. He was observed by George Stinson, a hotel porter who saw him with one boot on and one boot off. That summer night was particularly warm and the window had been thrown open as wide as possible to help circulate the stifling nocturnal air. His slumber, however, would be short-lived as he was awoken by the sound of children playing about outside. Their playful behaviour must have irritated Mr Bird immensely as he was seen throwing oranges at the rapscallions from his strategically advantageous first-floor position. This testimony was given by a widow named Mary Styles who lived in nearby Stanley Street. She had been walking down Dale Street when she had

Dale Street in modern times. The Alexandra Hotel no longer stands.

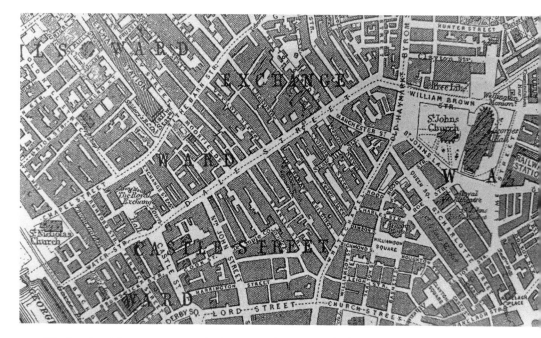

The barrister's last moments took place on Dale Street in the heart of the city centre.

heard the commotion and looked up to see the drunken barrister at the window with his hands in his pockets retrieving the missile-like fruit. He appeared to the witness to be someone who had just awoken from a heavy rest, in a semi-conscious state. As he approached the window further, Mary watched in horror as he fell through the opening head-first out into the night. She ran to his assistance but the body was lying lifeless on the ground. Mr Bird was rushed to hospital but he was already dead; the end being delivered through a decisive fracture in his spine. At a subsequent inquest it was heard that the thirty-two-year-old had been due to marry within the month and no doubt the news of his sad and accidental demise would be a bitter blow to his heartbroken fiancée.

34. Overcome

On 18 August 1899 a rather gruesome discovery was made at a Liverpool sugar refinery. On that Friday morning a fireman was working at the premises of Messrs Macfie and Sons in Tithebarn Street when he stumbled across a horrendously shocking sight. Behind one of the boilers, up against the flue, was the dead body of a man in a most horrific state. The corpse had shrivelled like a prune due to the intense heat, almost like an ancient mummy. These barely recognisable remains had belonged to fifty-two-year-old Richard Winch. Evidence from medical professionals suggested that the labourer had likely been overcome by fumes and fell unconscious, never to awaken. Death would have been painless.

Tithebarn Street has been transformed unrecognisably since its early years.

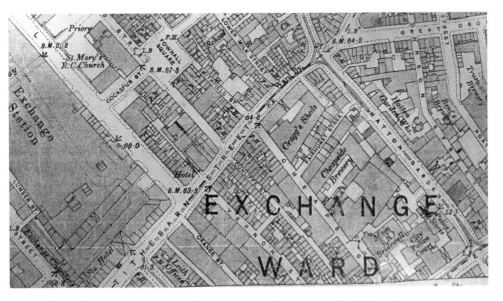

Richard Winch's remains were found at a factory in the vicinity of Tithebarn Street.

35. The Ghost Hunter

In September 1904 a young ghost hunter by the name of Hugh Morgan took it upon himself to investigate the world of spirit in the interests of his local community. Outside one ordinary but empty house in Everton's Field Street, a large and curious crowd had gathered. The property had gained a reputation for being haunted and much interest was given to the supposed supernatural goings-on within. Hugh was particularly intrigued and was determined to gain an audience with the alleged spectre. He took it upon himself to climb over the back wall and smash a glass pane in order to grant himself admittance. On unfastening the latch to the back door he entered in search of the resident ghoul and bravely explored the vacant house. Outside, neighbours showed much excitement as to Morgan's fate and stood waiting and watching with baited breath. As Hugh crept from room to room a chilling sense of unease penetrated his every pore. He was not alone. The man felt heart-pounding fear like never before as the intrepid investigator soon came face to face with a mysterious, uniformed figure. It drew closer and closer, step by step and it was not long until Hugh felt a firm and unwelcome grip press down hard on his shoulder.

The site where a mysterious spectre was said to lurk.

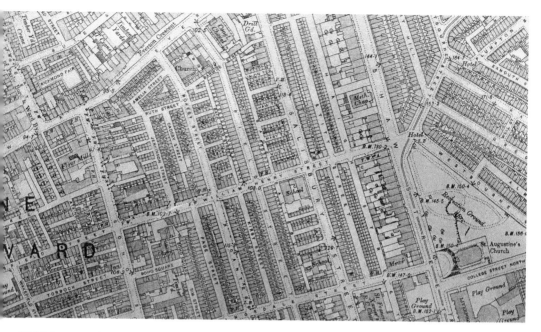

Field Street as shown on a map from 1893.

'You're under arrest' cried the 'ghost' and Hugh was later hauled before the stipendiary magistrate on a charge of breaking and entering.

'What business of yours was it to enter this house?' asked the magistrate.

'The house is haunted. I thought it was good for the landlord and good for the neighbourhood.'

'You must not break people's windows.'

'It is a haunted house, your Worship.'

The Court chuckled with laughter.

'What does that matter? Five shillings and costs or seven days' imprisonment. You can leave the ghost alone for a bit now!'

36. A Carbolic Conclusion

The shops of London Road seen in the 1920s.

In November 1897 an inquest was held into the sad circumstances surrounding the death of Thomas Herbert. It appeared that the twenty-nine-year old was usually a cheery man with a steady and happy disposition. On Monday 22 November he left his home in Kensington's Edinburgh Street, as was customary, to work at a shop in London Road where he was the manager. Staff at the premises recalled Thomas arriving for work early that day but saw him go out sometime before 9.00 a.m. that morning. He was never to return. It was only on the following morning that Thomas was discovered lying dead in the shop cellar. He had ended his life by downing a quantity of carbolic acid, a bottle of which was found at his side. Evidence provided by the shop owner revealed that Thomas' affairs were not quite in order and his papers were actually going through checks by auditors. It was an issue his employer regretfully had not yet the time to discuss. It was also revealed that Thomas took an overly keen interest in

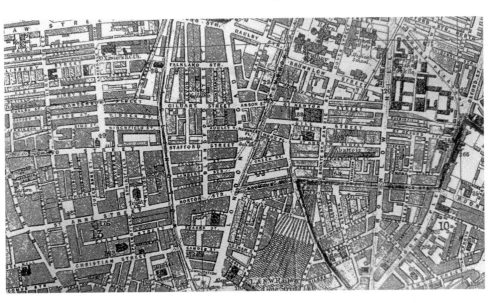

The suicide of Thomas Herbert took place in the busy commercial area of London Road.

the sporting pages and had frequent dealings with a money office. The jury returned a verdict of 'suicide whilst in a state of temporary mental derangement' with Coroner Sampson remarking that it was a great shame such poisons were so freely and readily available about the city.

37. Stand-off

A desperate skirmish came close to deadly tragedy back in December 1915 when a tense stand-off arose in a busy city street. That winter Henry Wilson, a native of the Caribbean island of Barbados was staying at a lodging house in Great George Square. Police had been called to the property to investigate an allegation of larceny and an officer was directed to the suspect's bedroom. On entering, Detective Howard witnessed Wilson in the act of tying his boots and demanded the man show him his registration papers, as required by law. With his boots laced tight Wilson replied 'I will get them for you' but no sooner had the sentence been uttered that Wilson was out the door taking the staircase at four steps at a time. Detective Howard raced after him and both men were seen running down the street, one in hot pursuit of the other. They were unaware of the danger that lay in wait. The young Barbadian could see no way out and from his pocket he pulled out a revolver, fully loaded, and pointed it straight at

Great George Square, where the stand-off took place.

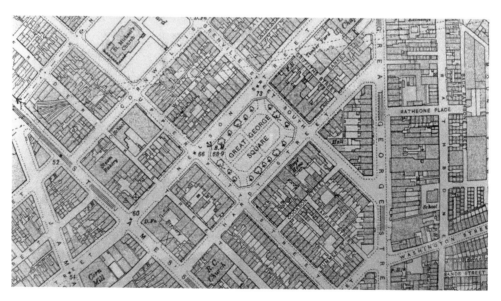

Great George Square depicted on a map from the early 1900s.

the policeman's head. The anxious scene attracted the attention of many traumatised onlookers who heard Wilson threaten the officer, screaming that if he came any closer he would shoot. Liverpool came close to losing another of its brave law enforcers that afternoon but with the assistance of boarding house owner Gustav Homburg and a valiant member of the public, the situation was brought to an end. Wilson was tackled to the ground and the weapon successfully removed from his grasp without injury.

He was later brought before the city stipendiary and was sentenced to two months imprisonment for assault and another month for having contravened the Defence of the Realm Act by bringing a revolver and cartridges into the UK without permission.

38. A Double Disaster

In November 1848 Liverpool was rocked by a double explosion which caused great alarm and unease to all in the neighbourhood. That shocking weekend saw Richard Jones hard at work in his shop at No. 58 Dale Street, plying his trade as an ironmonger. Like similar traders of the day gunpowder was frequently required in the course of his business, but Jones' health and safety procedures surrounding the matter left much to be desired. That afternoon a young and presumably naive employee by the name of Buckstone approached a whole canister of the stuff by means of candlelight. The inevitable consequences followed and a loud boom cried out as 30 lbs of gunpowder combusted in an instant. It sent shockwaves throughout the city and residents and merchants trembled with the force of the blast. Windows fell from their panes, properties quaked at their very foundations. The boy, a customer and Mr Jones himself were seriously injured in the explosion and as the fire spread throughout the store another canister set up in a window display suddenly began to spark. A second roaring boom rang out and glass was sent flying out into the street, showering the cobbles in hot glistening shards. The brigade was soon on the scene and during their efforts

The buildings of Dale Street were shook by the explosions.

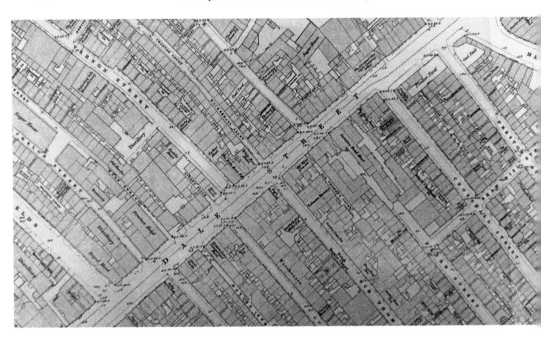

A mid-Victorian map showing the location of the double disaster.

one eagle-eyed officer observed a third canister had become enveloped with a sheet of burning canvas. It was removed with all due haste and placed in a cooling water tub. Later, after the commotion had ceased, this canister was found to contain a further 20 lbs of highly flammable gunpowder.

39. Cleaners Beware

On 16 October 1907, cleaning lady Mrs Craig was industriously dusting the ironwork surrounding the well of the lift in Water Street's Colonial House. Somewhat foolishly, the woman disregarded warnings not to clean the lift while it was in operation and retrieved a small stepladder to assist in her chores. She propped the ladder next to the contraption and proceeded to lean over the ironwork with her head inside the lift shaft. Tragically Mrs Creig's head was taken clean off as the lift suddenly began to descend from the floor above, cutting through the woman's neck as it did so.

Water Street as seen in the twenty-first century.

Water Street depicted on a map in the early years of the twentieth century.

40. A Doctor's Vengeance

Dr Patrick O'Callaghan was employed as an assistant to Dr Richard Ireland and had worked with him for around ten years. He rented a room from his employer and lived with the family at No. 2 Harlech Street, Walton. The summer of 1894 saw Dr Ireland take some much-needed rest and head off on holiday. Back home, his wife Mary asked her friend and neighbour Eleanor Sayers if she would like to stay with her for a few days for company until her husband returned home. On the night of 8 August the women, Mary's son William, Dr O'Callaghan, and a teenage servant by the name of Annie Washington were all inside the house. None of them suspected anything of the tragic events that would transpire later that evening.

The three adults had all been drinking for the better half of the day, with the doctor feeling very much the worse for it. Mary had been feeling unwell of late and had chosen to stay in bed for the majority of the afternoon. The doctor had been drinking in the parlour and by nightfall he could hardly stand. As midnight approached the household retired to bed and Eleanor went to fetch a final drink of ginger beer from the kitchen and to make sure the lights were switched off for the evening. She also poured a glass of milk for Mary who had remained upstairs in an ill, but tipsy, condition.

Eleanor had only descended the stairs for a moment when Dr O'Callaghan trudged into the master bedroom. He approached Mary, demanding more whiskey. She rebuked his request, stating that in his clearly intoxicated state he had had quite enough for one evening. In her own drunken frame of mind the woman then grabbed a glass tumbler and launched it over towards the drunkard, intending to frighten him off out of the room. Her aim was misjudged and the glass hit the doctor on the head, causing him to bleed and grimace in pain. He staggered out in a rage as he attempted to stem the flow from his brow.

A few moments later Mary heard a scream of terror. It was her son. 'Paddy! Paddy!' he cried, and the noise of a fall, followed by a crash of glass, echoed through the whole house. Mary immediately leapt out of bed all the while hearing her son call out in panic-stricken desperation. The two males shared a room and normally got on well, but who knew what upset could be caused through too much alcohol.

The door to Dr O'Callaghan's bedroom was open and by the light of a gas lamp Mrs Ireland noticed Dr O'Callaghan scrambling up off the floor. He had fallen during his unprovoked attack against the unarmed eleven-year-old, who was no match for the psychotic adult. Dr O'Callaghan got up and proceeded to beat the boy mercilessly, throwing him about the room like a ragdoll.

No. 2 Harlech Street, Walton – the unassuming house where the atrocity was committed.

Young Annie, the servant girl, occupied the small bedroom across the landing and she had been awoken by the sound of the unpleasant events. Her door was missing two glass panels which gave the thirteen-year-old a perfect but unenviable view of the activity therein. Shocked, she ran down the stairs and headed for the door. Annie ran outside, closely followed by Mary in search of a policeman. She eventually ran into PC Deacon, who hurried with Annie back to the house. He was met by Mary and Eleanor downstairs. Neither women seemed drunk to the officer, who judged Mary to be merely agitated and Eleanor in a silent state of shock.

He rushed upstairs and entered Dr O'Callaghan's room where he found the man lying on a bed in a state of undress. The officer was no sooner accosted by Mrs Ireland, 'where is my child; my darling infant?' she pleaded. The boy William was nowhere to be seen.

'I charge that woman with murderously assaulting me' slurred the doctor, as he pointed unsteadily from the pillow and nursed the wound to his head.

Constable Deacon's chief concern was for the boy. He searched the upper quarters of the house and in a small room removed a bed from a wall. Underneath he found the terrified child lying on his back with his intestines protruding from his bloodied torso. In the struggle a sharp implement had pierced the boy's abdomen and now his organs were exposed for all to see.

The officer carefully lifted the boy onto the bed before he was transported to Bootle Hospital for treatment for the ghastly protrusion.

Dr O'Callaghan's room meanwhile was a frenzied scene of mayhem. There were broken wooden chairs, broken panes of glass, a broken mirror and splatters of blood all across the floor. The doctor was also covered in the same, much of it due to the seeping wound upon his head.

The dishevelled man was promptly arrested and taken into custody where he was met by Sergeant Laing. 'I did not intend to do him any injury at all!' protested Dr O'Callaghan. 'I only pulled him out of bed to frighten the mother.'

At the hospital every possible notion was considered by medical practitioners but as the hours went by, each avenue proved hopeless. Death was an eventual certainty. Before peritonitis set in Dr Dickinson obtained a disposition from the boy who laid the blame squarely at the prisoner's door:

I am eleven years old. Late last night Dr O'Callaghan was kissing me. I asked the doctor to come up to bed and he came and then got out again. He commenced calling old things up about my mother and her family. He got hold of me and hammered me on the floor, and then fell on me, hurting his nose, and he blamed me for it. He hammered me around the room and on the broken chairs. I was knocked senseless. I tried several times to get away, and he followed me again and hammered me. I ran away and got under my father's bed and became quite senseless from fright. Then I heard my mother calling me, and then the police came. Mrs Sayers was asleep in bed in my mother's room. I wanted the doctor to come to bed as he was nagging my mother and she wanted to go to sleep as she didn't want to be kept awake all of the night.

William Ireland passed away on 14 August and was buried later that week at Anfield Cemetery. A great crowd descended upon the house to witness the funeral and pay their respects. Almost twenty officers were assigned to keep order as the mass of well-wishers walked alongside the hearse and gathered at the graveside.

Patrick O'Callaghan stood trial for murder at St George's Hall on 27 November. Mr Justice Collins was to determine his fate. After listening to the evidence he reminded the jury that it was not necessary to show that at the time of the occurrence the defendant had any deliberate intention of committing murder. If a person was in such a condition of mind that he was able to form an intention of doing serious harm to another person, then, if death ensued, drink or no drink, he was guilty of murder. It was necessary to show that the defendant intended to do grievous bodily harm to the boy.

The jury after only a few minutes of consideration declared that the prisoner was not guilty of the crime of murder, but instead guilty of the lesser charge of manslaughter.

It is a miserable thing to see a man of your education standing there in the dock, convicted of manslaughter caused by giving way, as you did give way, to drink, and to drink in the most terrible and degraded form. The jury have taken a merciful view of your case, but there cannot be the slightest doubt in the mind of anyone who has heard the case that this child met his death through your violence, violence that was continued for a considerable time, and violence that was of a very grave character.

The site of the macabre goings-on, depicted on a map from 1908.

The jury have no doubt, given weight to the fact that you were so drunk that they were able to come to the conclusion that you did not realise what you were doing, but nothing can excuse the brutality that you showed on this occasion, which led to the death of this child. You must go to penal servitude for twelve years.

41. The Hotel Jumper

On 2 June 1891 the city coroner heard details regarding the very public demise of William Gilchrist who passed away earlier that weekend. At around 3.00 a.m. the previous Sunday, Dr Hamilton received an urgent message to get to the North Western Hotel on Lime Street. A guest was showing signs of acute mania and needed urgent medical attention. Mr Gilchrist was behaving very noisily and acting in a most irrational manner. He had arrived at the hotel two days earlier from the West Coast of Africa and complained he was suffering from malarial fever. He appeared to be between thirty-five and forty years of age and his luggage suggested connections to Edinburgh.

Dr Hamilton stayed with the man for some considerable time and eventually managed to calm him down. He then telephoned for a male nurse to assist in looking after the man overnight. John Gannon, an invalid's attendant attached to the Hope

Lime Street and the North Western Hotel from where the manic guest fell to his death.

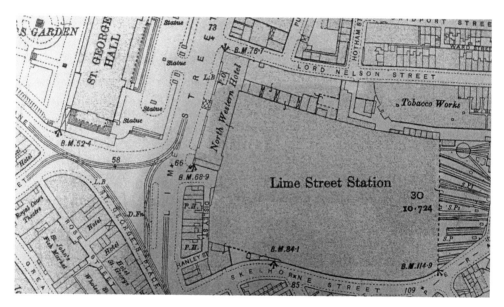

The North Western Hotel stands adjacent to Lime Street Station in the city centre.

Street Nurses' Institution arrived at the hotel at around 5.00 a.m. He was directed to the patient's bedroom on the fourth floor and spoke with the doctor, who promised that he would call again after breakfast. He advised that John should stay with the man and keep a close eye on him. The doctor was inclined to believe Mr Gilchrist's unusual behaviour was brought about through alcohol, but he felt unable to say for sure. In his passion the patient had bitten his tongue so badly that it was difficult to form a definite diagnosis.

As the hours passed, the man sat in a chair chatting pleasantly enough to the nurse. During their conversation Mr Gilchrest suddenly shot up, grabbed a beer bottle and used it to smash a hole through the hotel window. The window was some way up, so much so Doctor Hamilton thought it safe not to have the man moved to another room. The distressed guest heaved himself up and out of the shattered opening and stuck his head and shoulders out into the fresh morning air. John Gannon leapt up after him and summoned all his power to drag the man back into the room. 'Help!' he shouted, but Mr Gilchrist was struggling too hard and forced his way further and further out from his hopeful saviour's grasp.

Driver Thomas Armson was sitting in his cab outside the building when he heard the unmistakable sound of shattering glass. He looked up to see a restless figure squirming through the broken pane, held back only by one leg. Open-mouthed, the cab driver could do nothing but watch as the man scrambled further out onto the windowsill before plummeting 70 feet towards the ground. He hit the pavement with an almighty thud. Early morning pedestrians rushed to his assistance. Among them was a police constable who was on duty in Lime Street. 'Don't go officer' wheezed Mr Gilchrest, alive, but only just, 'there is a man going to murder me.'

The mysterious jumper was taken to the Northern Hospital where he died of his injuries a short time later.

In summing up the astonishing events of that dreadful morning, the coroner declared that William Gilchrest died from the effects of injuries caused by his having thrown himself from the hotel bedroom window into the street while in a state of mental derangement, but apparently without any suicidal intentions.

42. A Botched Job

A deplorable discovery was made on 19 May 1891. The vile evidence pointed to a despicable case of murder and mutilation. That night a dock gateman observed a bag floating in the waters of the Sandon Dock and on taking it out was horrified to find the body of a youth aged ten with his throat cut from ear to ear, and both legs sawn off at the knee. The knife and saw with which the deed had been done were also in the bag. Police discovered that the disfigured remains were that of a boy by the name of Nicholas Martin who had gone missing from his home in Bridgewater Street the previous weekend. A further clue came in the form of a slip of brown paper, partly torn, which had been left in the bag along with the body parts. This bore the stamp of the Seaman and Fireman's Union who had their office situated at No. 19 Stanhope Street. A search of the premises revealed that this was the scene of grossly inhuman activity, with considerable traces of blood found upon the floorboards. Underneath, experts had found dust soaked in the very same. It was surmised that the deceased had been beaten about the face until unconscious before meeting his end by the razor. This would account for the lack of spurting or violent gushing of blood

The once feared site of Kirkdale Prison has seen been turned into a playground.

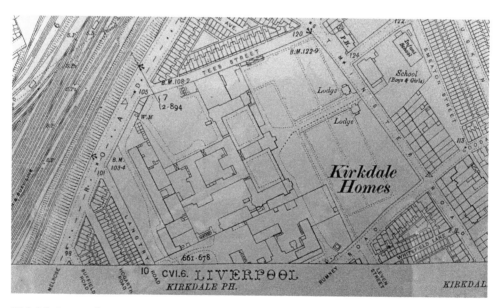

Kirkdale Prison shown on a map from the turn of the twentieth century.

as otherwise expected. The perpetrator of this mad act was John Conway, aka Owen Giblinth, sixty-one years of age and secretary of the Seaman and Fireman's Union. Before Judge Smith and a jury of his peers, Conway was found guilty of murder and sentenced to hang.

Kirkdale Gaol was the setting for what was to be an historic punishment, one so gruesome as to be etched into the minds of all in attendance.

On the morning of his execution the condemned man wrote a letter of admission to be read once the sentence had been carried out. The public executioner James Berry had travelled to Liverpool to conduct the proceedings, but he appeared to be in a disagreeable mood and rude to prison officials. Conway was positioned onto the scaffold and after a few final words, the order was given. Father Bronte then read out the confession:

I accept the sentence that has been pronounced against me as just, and I now offer my life in satisfaction to all whom I have offended - to God, to my religion, to my country, to the parents of the victim, to the victim, himself and to society. In confessing my guilt I protest that my motive was not outrage, such a thought I never in all my life entertained drink has been my ruin, not lust. I was impelled to the crime while under the influence of drink by a fit of murderous mania and a morbid curiosity to observe the process of dying. A moment after the commission of the crime I experienced the deepest sorrow for it, and would have done anything in the world to undo it. May God in his mercy forgive me.

John Conway, 20 August 1891

However, his eloquent delivery was adulterated by the sound of blood trickling into the pit of the gallows. The prisoner's head had been almost torn from the body and was merely hanging from the muscles of his neck. 'Take them out!' seethed Berry, referring to the news reporters who had peered in for a closer look. The media was rushed out of the scaffold room and away from the sickening sight. It was customary for reporters to stay until life had been declared extinct, but on this occasion that outcome was obvious.

When Berry vacated the room and met with reporters he complained that prison staff would have given Conway another 8 inches if it wasn't for his intervention and probably would have been decapitated completely. He seemed anxious that the reporters should say nothing public about the matter, but the grisly details were far too salacious to remain concealed.

At an inquest into the incident it was believed that Conway's death must have been instantaneous, owing not only to the fracture of the neck but to the bursting of the blood vessels. Looked at from the brink of the scaffold, the rope was hidden deep in the man's neck and his flesh seemed to have given way like a rotten garment under the sudden strain. It was also alleged that Conway had been too tightly pinioned by the hangman, not just causing him discomfort but physical pain. The botched execution of John Conway and rumours of unprofessionalism proved to be of great embarrassment for the Government who already had their doubts about Berry after a series of other miscalculations. It was privately agreed that he should be removed from the post, but Berry resigned the following year after a career involving 131 executions.

43. No. 21 Abercromby Square

The Georgian houses of Abercromby Square are some of the most beautiful and historic properties in the whole of Liverpool. Back in 1852, however, No. 21 was to be the scene of a most terrible and shocking incident. On 20 March twenty-three-year-old Alice Shaw was, as usual, at work. She was a domestic servant employed by the prosperous Ripley family. They had made a considerable sum through Thomas Ripley's East Indian trade links, he being one of the very first merchants to work with China. Mr Ripley shared his large and regal home with Julia his wife and their several maids, with the young Alice being one of them. She had been employed by the couple for around six years and on that cold spring morning she had eaten her breakfast before going upstairs to start her daily chores. For the past few days Miss Shaw had complained of feeling slightly unwell and it was on this day that her symptoms reached their dramatic climax. At around 1.00 p.m. Margaret Naylor, a fellow servant, went to her bedroom and to her great surprise found Alice lying sedately on the floorboards. 'Alice? Alice?' There was no response. In abject fear she shouted for the cook, Margaret Massey to come and help. 'Alice are you ok?' Again, Miss Shaw lay there like a zombie in some sort of dream-like state. With Miss Massey's assistance the two women managed to place Alice in the comfort of a bed where she remained in her state of complete

Abercromby Square is now largely populated with students of the University of Liverpool.

insensibility. Things were not looking good 'Fetch the mistress!' cried the maid. Miss Massey hurried downstairs to find Mrs Ripley. She contacted a physician with great urgency and Dr James Nottage soon arrived at the house and admitted without delay. He raced up the stairs and examined the poor woman, upon whom peculiar stains of blood covered both of her hands. 'See if you can find anything to explain these marks in Miss Shaw's room' said the doctor. Further examination took place as the housemaid rushed into Alice's room to see if she could find any explanation for the crimson marks. In the half-filled washbasin there lay the floating body of a newborn baby girl. It was quite dead and showed no signs of life as it bobbed about the water. Around its neck there sat a flannel handkerchief tied tightly, wrapped around twice. The cook let out a spine-tingling scream and almost in tears told the doctor what she had found. Dr Nottage calmed the panic-stricken woman down and asked to be directed to the discovery. He found the corpse of a baby girl face down in the water, complete with an uncut umbilical cord. He recoiled upon noticing in the utensil cupboard nearby, the bloody placenta. Moments later he conducted an in-depth, silent examination of Alice Shaw, asking no questions to the dumbstruck woman. He found that she had indeed recently delivered a child and there was little doubt that it was the same infant that now lay dead in the sink. He had no choice but to inform the authorities who arrested Alice on suspicion of murder. She was placed under house arrest and prevented from leaving No. 21 Abercromby Square until further notice.

Dr Nottage took the body away to be inspected and he later conducted a thorough post-mortem. He concluded that the child had been born alive. The tongue of the infant was heavily swollen and partly exposed hanging from its mouth. It was his

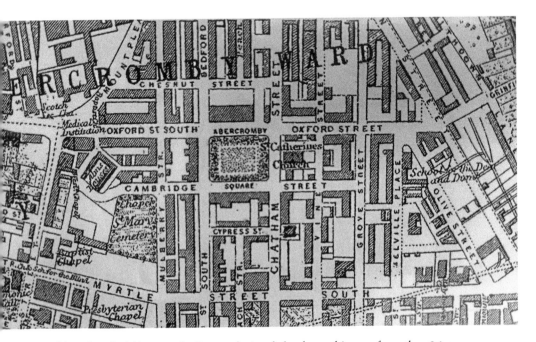

The neighbourhood of Abercromby Square depicted clearly on this map from the 1860s.

learned view that this was due to some serious pressure being applied to the back of the girl's head, pressing down deep in the water perhaps. Dr Nottage was of the firm belief the child had died due to suffocation from its immersion in the water and that her death was almost impossible in any other way without the mother's involvement. It was this evidence that convinced the Coroner's Court of Miss Shaw's guilty intent and she was sent to stand trial at the assizes as soon as she was judged medically able. It was a whole five months before Alice stood before Justice Campbell on a charge of murdering her newly born illegitimate daughter and to discern her ultimate fate. Again, Dr Nottage gave his evidence with which Mr Preston prosecuted; his key point being that the child was proved to be born alive due to the air in its lungs causing it to float. It was Mr Monk for the defence who challenged the physician's conclusions with great skill. It was his opinion that the air in the lungs may have been breathed by the child before she had been actually born. This quite plausible possibility was enough to throw enough considerable doubt into the case and prevented the arrival of a guilty verdict. After a short consultation, and despite the presence of a flannel handkerchief tied around the child's neck, the jury found Alice Shaw not guilty of her charge of infanticide.

44. Suicide at The Beehive

On 12 March 1898 the Liverpool coroner Mr Sampson held an inquest into the death of Duncan Owens, a twenty-two-year-old billiard marker from Lamb Street. Until recently his job had involved him keeping the scores at billiard games, but six months ago he had lost his post and become quite down about being unable to find similar work. The week before his death Duncan had drank from the Sunday through to the Thursday in attempt to drown his depressed spirits and block out the abysmal world as he knew it. He had been able to secure a job as a barman at a pub in King Street, but this was not to his satisfaction and seemed to just worsen his already deep sense of unhappiness. At about noon the previous Friday, Mr Owens was at work at the public house, but as was his intemperance of late, was inebriated having been drinking on the job. The landlord became most irate and told him to go home and sober up. This was a warning; another stunt like this then Duncan would be out of a position. He gathered his things and left.

At around 12.50 p.m. the young man stepped into the Beehive Hotel in Paradise Street where licensee George Bell was serving behind the bar. He thought Mr Owens to be quite sober, if only a little melancholy when he ordered a shot of whiskey. Mr Bell poured him a small glass. 'Could I have some hot water please?' asked Duncan, 'I'm not feeling very well and want to take a powder to settle my stomach.' 'Certainly,' replied Mr Bell, and he poured him a second glass brimming with water. Duncan then

The place where Duncan Owens took his final breath remains a busy public house.

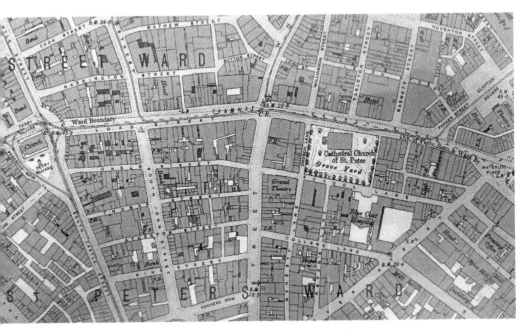

The Beehive public house as seen on a map from the late nineteenth century.

began to mix a powder by tossing the contents from one glass to the other and stirring it around. He took a firm grip of the glass and gulped down the mixture in several dogged slurps. Mr Owens wiped his mouth, then left the bar heading to the gents toilets where he remained for some time. The curious Mr Bell started to become concerned and after several minutes inspected the lavatory to see if the man was alright. He found Duncan on the floor in a most depressed state of mind. 'Sir, are you ill?' asked George kneeling over his customer. 'No, I have taken oxalic acid. I don't want to live.'

George rushed out into the street and implored a police constable to come and help the dying man. He attempted to administer some emetics to cleanse Duncan's stomach, but these failed to have any effect. Soon a horse ambulance drew up outside the pub to take Mr Owens to hospital, but it was already too late. Duncan passed away while being loaded into the ambulance as medics stood helpless, unable to do anything else than to place a respectful sheet over the dead man's body. An inquest concluded that the young man had committed suicide while of unsound mind.